HTML & JavaScript
Programming Concepts

E. Shane Turner
MCI Senior Software Engineer, Colorado Springs, CO

Karl Barksdale
Technology Consultant, Provo, UT

JOIN US ON THE INTERNET
WWW: http://www.thomson.com   A service of I(T)P®

South-Western Educational Publishing
an International Thomson Publishing company I(T)P®

Cincinnati • Albany, NY • Belmont, CA • Bonn • Boston • Detroit • Johannesburg • London • Madrid
Melbourne • Mexico City • New York • Paris • Singapore • Tokyo • Toronto • Washington

Team Leader: Karen Schmohe
Managing Editor: Carol Volz
Editor: Mark Cheatham
Art Coordinator: Mike Broussard
Consulting Editor: Mary Todd
Production House: Litten Editing and Production
Marketing Managers: Larry Qualls, Steve Wright
Internal Design: Anne Small
Cover Design: Lou Ann Thesing

ISBN: 0-538-68822-X

3 4 5 6 7 8 9 10 BC 05 04 03 02 01 00

Printed in the United States of America

I(T)P®
International Thomson Publishing

South-Western Educational Publishing is a division of International
Thomson Publishing, Inc. The ITP® registered trademark is used
under license.

The names of all commercially available software mentioned herein
are used for identification purposes only and may be trademarks
or registered trademarks of their respective owners. South-Western
Educational Publishing disclaims any affiliation, association, connection with, sponsorship, or endorsement by such owners.

Using This Book

Introduction

Section Openers provide a brief overview of each chapter and are written in a conversational style that is easy to understand.

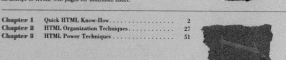

HTML, the Doorway to JavaScript

Welcome to HTML, the doorway to JavaScript.

HTML is a funny acronym coming from the words **Hypertext Markup Language**. HTML started a communications revolution in the 1990s, changing the way we live, communicate, and interact with each other.

HTML is made up of little tags, like this:

(CENTER) (/CENTER)

HTML tags tell a Web browser, like Netscape's Navigator or Microsoft's Internet Explorer, how to display Web pages. These tags accompany Web pages along the journey from their home bases on Web servers to the people who want to see them all over the world. Without HTML, the World Wide Web never would have been created.

JavaScripts couldn't exist without HTML either. JavaScripts catch rides on HTML Web pages as they blast at the speed of an electron along the Web. JavaScripts ride along on Web pages like satellites ride inside the cargo bay of the space shuttle into deep space. When the HTML shuttle arrives at your Web browser, an electronic door is opened with a special (JAVASCRIPT) tag, and JavaScripts go to work.

When HTML tags and JavaScripts arrive at your Web browser, magical things can happen. Pictures can move, sounds can play, questions can be answered interactively, and people can learn new things in new ways. The power of JavaScript and the power of HTML combine to make the Web a great place to visit.

HTML was invented by Tim Berners-Lee, a researcher in Switzerland working for CERN (the European Laboratory for Particle Physics). He found a way people in distant locations can communicate and share information together.

JavaScript was created a few years later by Netscape Communications Corporation. Netscape decided that they wanted to add more power to HTML Web pages, so they invented JavaScript.

JavaScript is similar to a programming language called **Java**, but there are important differences. Java requires some very sophisticated software to prepare Java programs called applets. JavaScript can be typed directly into a word processor the same way HTML is entered. JavaScript is just the ticket to add exciting capabilities to Web pages without the fuss of a traditional programming system.

Before you can use JavaScript successfully, you will need an understanding of how HTML works. This knowledge will help you link JavaScript to HTML Web pages for maximum effect.

Quick HTML Know-How

Chapter Objectives

In this chapter, you will learn about HTML tags. After reading Chapter 1, you will be able to

1. discover HTML tags.
2. enter your starting tags.
3. learn to save correctly.
4. integrate levels of headings into Web pages.
5. create unordered, ordered, and embedded lists.

HTML Terms

angle brackets
home page
HTML
HTML page
Hypertext Markup Language
Internet Explorer
Java
JavaScript
Mosaic
Netscape Navigator
VRML
Web browser
Web page
Web site
Webmasters
welcome page

Communicating on the Web

HTML, or Hypertext Markup Language, allows you to create Web pages. HTML organizes documents and tells Web browsers how Web pages should look on your computer screen. The colors, pictures, and backgrounds on Web pages are determined by HTML tags.

HTML tags work with any Web browser. If you create an HTML page, and do it correctly, your Web browser can read it. In fact, HTML is the official language of the World Wide Web. While there are many other languages spoken in cyberspace (like **Java**, **VRML**, and **JavaScript**), HTML is the most widely used.

HTML tags work everywhere on the Web. HTML tags display HTML pages on Macintosh or Windows computers. They work on UNIX and Sun Computers. They even work on Web television sets and on portable phones.

HTML tags are so simple that anyone can learn a few of the essential tags quickly. They usually appear in pairs enclosed in **angle brackets**. These brackets can be found on the comma and period keys on your keyboard. Press the Shift key to create them.

To more clearly understand how tags work, analyze this example. If you want to center the title of this book on a Web page, you can write:

(CENTER)HTML and JavaScript(/CENTER)

Chapter Opener

Chapter Openers provide Objectives, Terms, and an introduction to chapter content. Each chapter builds upon the skills and understanding learned in previous chapters.

Activities

Activities are written to support each chapter objective. These activities cover the Web programming topics that are most relevant to today's classroom and workplace. Each activity begins with a brief explanation of key concepts.

Step-by-Step Instructions provide hands-on reinforcement and simplify the process of working through each activity.

ACTIVITY 2.2

Objective:
In this activity, you will learn to change the background color of your Web page, and you will create lines of varying width and length using attributes and values.

Figure 2.5
Changing background colors

Lines and Background Colors

Attributes and Values

HTML tags can be enhanced by giving them **attributes** and **values**. Take the ⟨BODY⟩ tag. You can add elements to the body tag that will dramatically change the look of your Web page. For example, to change the background color of your Web page, you can add the background attribute command and give the tag a color value, as shown in Figure 2.5.

Try it!

1. Open your *Seven.html* file.

Body Tag   Attribute

⟨BODY **BGCOLOR=YELLOW**⟩

Reminder for Notepad users: Don't forget to select the *Word Wrap* option from the *Edit* menu when you open the file.

2. Enter BGCOLOR=YELLOW inside the BODY tag near the top of your Web page, as shown in bold in Figure 2.5.

3. Save your work as *Eight.html*.

4. View these changes in your Web browser. Your page should turn yellow.

5. Experiment. Change the attribute to BLUE, GREEN, RED, WHITE, or another color of your choice.

NET FACT

Hexadecimal Colors

Computers speak only in numbers. Values are expressed as numbers that the computer understands. Color values can be carefully controlled and changed to match virtually every color in the rainbow by using the hexadecimal values for certain colors.

Hexadecimal digits operate on a base-16 number system rather than the base-10 number system we humans normally use. Hexadecimal numbers use the letters A, B, C, D, E, and F along with the numbers 0 to 9 to create their 16 different digits.

For example, look at the following color values expressed as numbers:

White = #FFFFFF   Green = #00FF00
Black = #000000   Blue   = #0000FF
Red   = #FF0000   Yellow = #FFFF00

Shades of these colors are created by changing the numbers. For example, a really great sky blue can be created on your HTML page with the number 00CCFF. Do you want a nice light purple? Try FF95FF. An ugly slime green can be created with AAFF00.

Substitute text color values with numbers in your Web page and see what happens. For example, try this:

BGCOLOR=#AAFF00 VLINK=#FF95FF TEXT=#00CCFF LINK=#FFFF00

Sidebar Features

Special Features occur throughout the text to present important concepts in a brief, easy to read format.

NET FACT

Net Fact presents important technical information.

 Netiquette discusses the common practices within the online community.

Net Ethics

Net Ethics provides a forum for discussion of important ethical and legal concerns in relation to the Internet.

Internet Milestone

Internet Milestone presents significant historical benchmarks in the development of the Internet.

End-Of-Chapter

Net Vocabulary reinforces key concepts presented in the text in the form of a vocabulary exercise.

Net Review short answer questions test the retention of important chapter information. This serves as an excellent review for the chapter test.

NET VOCABULARY

Define the following terms:

1. attributes
2. fonts
3. hexadecimal

4. HTTP
5. hyperlinks
6. hypertext links

7. Hypertext Transfer Protocol
8. values

NET REVIEW

Give a short answer to the following questions:

1. What tag will make words FLASH on and off repeatedly?

2. What hexadecimal value will create the color yellow?

Net PROJect

CREATING AN ONLINE SURVEY

Great Applications, Inc. wants to enter the online video game business. However, before it starts programming the next great online video game, it wants to survey potential customers to see what kinds of online games they want to play and buy.

Brainstorm 10 questions that will help Great Applications learn what its customers want in a video game program. Use your ⟨FORM⟩ tag skills, and create an online survey to gather information from potential customers. Have your survey ask for the respondent's name and email address. Ask questions that utilize drop down lists, radio selection items, and checkboxes.

NET PROJECT TEAMWORK   A Table Tour

Great Applications, Inc. is asking your team to plan a world tour to demonstrate its new software video games to people in five major cities. You and your team have been asked to create a calendar of events for the tour using ⟨TABLE⟩ tags. The tour must be conducted during a single month and should involve five major cities.

When you create your calendar, create links to tourist information about the cities that you will be visiting on the tour. Use cell padding and cell borders to make the table interesting. You can even put pictures in the cells to illustrate the five cities you have selected for the software rollout.

To save some time, borrow the calendar you created in the *Thinking About Technology* section in Activity 3.4. Modify these tags to fit this exercise.

WRITING ABOUT TECHNOLOGY

Before you complete this section on HTML and move on to JavaScript, evaluate the impact and importance of HTML on worldwide communications and the economy.

How important is the WWW and HTML to the world's economy?

Net Project puts the user's new tools and skills to work by applying them to an ongoing Web-based business project.

Net Project Teamwork is a team option for the Net Project designed to emphasize the importance of working in teams to accomplish common goals.

Writing About Technology emphasizes the importance of developing writing and critical thinking skills within the emerging, complex world of Web computing. Each of these end-of-chapter assignments provides an opportunity for building a personal portfolio.

Net Fun

If you are interested in learning more about HTML, you can order HTML books right over the Web. A great place to visit is amazon.com. Amazon.com is the largest bookstore on the World Wide Web. If you can't find the book you are looking for at amazon.com, it probably doesn't exist. Read more about Amazon.com in the Internet Milestone report, *Business on the Web*, p. 65.

Net Fun is intended to show that with the Internet, it *is* possible to learn and have fun at the same time!

Everyone knows how popular the Internet has become over the past few years, but very few people know why. The hardware and software technologies that make the Internet work have been in existence for well over two decades. So why did it suddenly become an overnight success just recently?

More than any other technology, the Internet owes its tremendous success to the introduction of HyperText Markup Language (HTML). HTML is the backbone of the World Wide Web, and it is the primary mechanism used to distribute data across the information superhighway. Learning the capabilities and the structure of HTML is an essential step for anyone who would like to create colorful, eye-catching Web pages like those developed by professional Webmasters. Fortunately, HTML is relatively easy to learn, can be created with a standard text editor or word processor, and works with nearly any type of computer system. In short, it is difficult to imagine a better technology for you to explore. You will build both confidence and useful computer skills very quickly.

Despite its many wonderful qualities, however, HTML is a limited language. There are many useful tasks that simply cannot be accomplished with HTML alone, so many professional Web pages make use of some supplemental technology. Although there are several different technologies available that can extend the base functionality of HTML, there is no better choice for you than Java-Script. Like HTML, JavaScript can be created without the use of complex or expensive development software. In fact, JavaScript source code is typed directly into the appropriate HTML Web page file by means of a standard text editor or word processor. But perhaps the most valuable characteristic of the JavaScript language is that it is built upon solid, object-oriented programming concepts. This means that you not only can acquire impressive programming skills quickly, but you can also apply these skills to several other popular programming languages, such as Java, C++, or even Pascal.

HTML & JavaScript: Programming Concepts is evenly divided into two sections, each of which contains three chapters. The first section is devoted entirely to standard HTML and will provide you with a solid foundation for developing high-quality Web pages. The second section addresses the JavaScript language and will teach you how to integrate JavaScript source code with HTML in order to enhance the capabilities of your Web pages. Each of the six chapters presents several HTML/JavaScript concepts and then provides five hands-on programming activities to give you concrete examples of how these concepts can be applied to actual Web pages. A brief summary of these six chapters follows.

- *Chapter 1: Quick HTML Know-How* contains an introduction to HyperText Markup Language. This chapter will teach you what HTML tags are and how to create ordered and unordered lists in a Web page. It also covers some basic file management techniques to ensure that you can save and retrieve HTML document files correctly.

- *Chapter 2: HTML Organization Techniques* focuses on several HTML tags that can be used to organize information on a Web page. These tags give you the ability to adjust line spacing, add horizontal dividing lines, set the background color, set text colors, and create various kinds of hyperlinks.
- *Chapter 3: HTML Power Techniques* discusses several advanced HTML tags that provide the means to greatly enhance the appearance of Web pages. Using these tags, you can control the size, style, and color of fonts; include graphic images; organize data in tables; turn images into hyperlinks; and use different types of user input components to create electronic forms.
- *Chapter 4: What Is JavaScript?* explains the history and purpose of JavaScript and shows how JavaScript is integrated into an HTML Web page. This chapter also defines several essential JavaScript terms and describes some of the most basic parts of JavaScript syntax, including keywords, operators, objects, and methods.
- *Chapter 5: Using Images with JavaScript* shows you how to use graphic images in conjunction with JavaScript events and functions to add some impressive visual effects to a Web page. These effects include image rollovers, hyperlink rollovers, cycling ad banners, random image displays, and electronic slide shows.
- *Chapter 6: Creating Forms with JavaScript* builds on the introduction to forms presented in Chapter 3. It demonstrates how JavaScript can be used to enhance the functionality of HTML forms. This chapter will teach you how to lay out an electronic form, validate user input data, and provide the user with appropriate feedback.

ACKNOWLEDGEMENTS

The authors of this book would like to thank Mark Cheatham at South-Western Educational Publishing for managing this project from start to finish. We would also like to thank Malvine at Litten Editing and Production for coordinating the page layout of this book, and Mary at Todd Publishing Services for her superb editing skills.

E. Shane Turner would like to acknowledge Laura, Anthony, Diana, and Katie for letting me know how "cool" they think this book is. I would also like to express my gratitude to Stephani, Afton, Evan, Roman, and Emma for the many sacrifices they have had to make throughout the lifetime of this project. I love you all dearly.

Karl Barksdale would like to thank Hilary, Cory, and Marriette for their ongoing encouragement and support through this project and many others.

Karl Barksdale
E. Shane Turner

CONTENTS

SECTION 2—THE EXCITING WORLD OF JAVASCRIPT   72

CHAPTER 4
What Is JavaScript?   74

CHAPTER 5
Using Images with JavaScript   98

CHAPTER 6
Creating Forms with JavaScript   124

Hardware and Browser Software Requirements

HTML & JavaScript: Programming Concepts may be used with any computer system that supports a compatible Web browser. In order to be compatible, the browser must support version 1.1 of the JavaScript language specification.

Compatible browsers include:
- Netscape Navigator 3.0 or higher
- Microsoft Internet Explorer 3.0 or higher

Computer systems that support these Web browsers include:
- PCs running Microsoft Windows
- Macintosh systems
- UNIX workstations

Text Editor or Word Processing Software

Additional software requirements are simply a text editor or word processor for creating HTML and JavaScript source code such as Notepad (Windows), SimpleText (Mac), Microsoft Word, WordPerfect, WordPro, ClarisWorks, or even Microsoft Works.

HTML, the Doorway to JavaScript

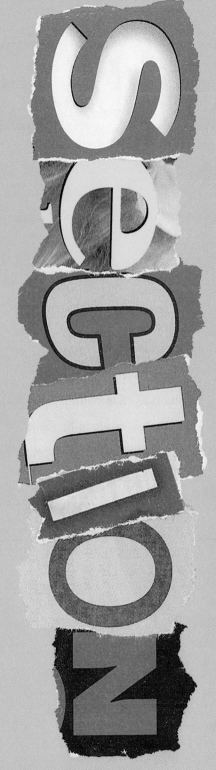

Welcome to HTML, the doorway to JavaScript.

HTML is a funny acronym coming from the words **Hypertext Markup Language**. HTML started a communications revolution in the 1990s, changing the way we live, communicate, and interact with each other.

HTML is made up of little tags, like this:

⟨CENTER⟩ ⟨/CENTER⟩

HTML tags tell a Web browser, like Netscape's Navigator or Microsoft's Internet Explorer, how to display Web pages. These tags accompany Web pages along the journey from their home bases on Web servers to the people who want to see them all over the world. Without HTML, the World Wide Web never would have been created.

JavaScripts couldn't exist without HTML either. JavaScripts catch rides on HTML Web pages as they blast at the speed of an electron along the Web. JavaScripts ride along on Web pages like satellites ride inside the cargo bay of the space shuttle into deep space. When the HTML shuttle arrives at your Web browser, an electronic door is opened with a special ⟨JAVASCRIPT⟩ tag, and JavaScripts go to work.

When HTML tags and JavaScripts arrive at your Web browser, magical things can happen. Pictures can move, sounds can play, questions can be answered interactively, and people can learn new things in new ways. The power of JavaScript and the power of HTML combine to make the Web a great place to visit.

HTML was invented by Tim Berners-Lee, a researcher in Switzerland working for CERN (the European Laboratory for Particle Physics). He found a way people in distant locations can communicate and share information together.

JavaScript was created a few years later by Netscape Communications Corporation. Netscape decided that they wanted to add more power to HTML Web pages, so they invented JavaScript.

JavaScript is similar to a programming language called **Java**, but there are important differences. Java requires some very sophisticated software to prepare Java programs called **applets**. JavaScript can be typed directly into a word processor the same way HTML is entered. JavaScript is just the ticket to add exciting capabilities to Web pages without the fuss of a traditional programming system.

Before you can use JavaScript successfully, you will need an understanding of how HTML works. This knowledge will help you link JavaScript to HTML Web pages for maximum effect.

Quick HTML Know-How

Chapter Objectives

In this chapter, you will learn about HTML tags. After reading Chapter 1, you will be able to

1 discover HTML tags.

2 enter your starting tags.

3 learn to save correctly.

4 integrate levels of headings into Web pages.

5 create unordered, ordered, and embedded lists.

HTML Terms

angle brackets

home page

HTML

HTML page

Hypertext Markup Language

Internet Explorer

Java

JavaScript

Mosaic

Netscape Navigator

VRML

Web browser

Web page

Web site

Webmasters

welcome page

Communicating on the Web

HTML, or Hypertext Markup Language, allows you to create Web pages. HTML organizes documents and tells Web browsers how Web pages should look on your computer screen. The colors, pictures, and backgrounds on Web pages are determined by HTML tags.

HTML tags work with any Web browser. If you create an HTML page, and do it correctly, your Web browser can read it. In fact, HTML is the official language of the World Wide Web. While there are many other languages spoken in cyberspace (like **Java, VRML**, and **JavaScript**), HTML is the most widely used.

HTML tags work everywhere on the Web. HTML tags display HTML pages on Macintosh or Windows computers. They work on UNIX and Sun Computers. They even work on Web television sets and on portable phones.

HTML tags are so simple that anyone can learn a few of the essential tags quickly. They usually appear in pairs enclosed in **angle brackets**. These brackets can be found on the comma and period keys on your keyboard. Press the Shift key to create them.

To more clearly understand how tags work, analyze this example. If you want to center the title of this book on a Web page, you can write:

⟨CENTER⟩HTML and JavaScript⟨/CENTER⟩

Notice that there is a starting tag, ⟨CENTER⟩, and a closing tag, ⟨/CENTER⟩. The only difference between the two tags is a slash / following the first angle bracket in the closing tag. The tags, ⟨CENTER⟩ ⟨/CENTER⟩, form a pair of tags. And if you haven't guessed already, these tags are called "center" tags. Anything between these tags will be centered on the page. Anything outside of the tags will not be affected by the command. It can't get any simpler than that! ■

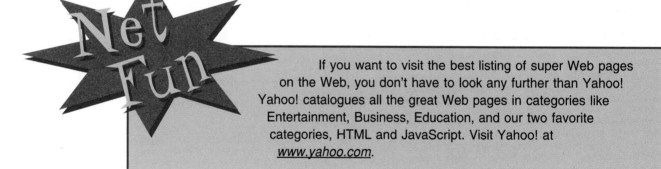

If you want to visit the best listing of super Web pages on the Web, you don't have to look any further than Yahoo! Yahoo! catalogues all the great Web pages in categories like Entertainment, Business, Education, and our two favorite categories, HTML and JavaScript. Visit Yahoo! at *www.yahoo.com*.

ACTIVITY

1.1

Objective:
In this activity, you will learn to view HTML source tags.

Uncover the Page Beneath the Page

The Web is full of Web pages. Some are very interesting, some are very exciting, some are too busy, and some are dull and boring.

It doesn't matter if a page is interesting or dull; all pages have some very similar characteristics. Let's see what we mean.

Look at Figure 1.1a.

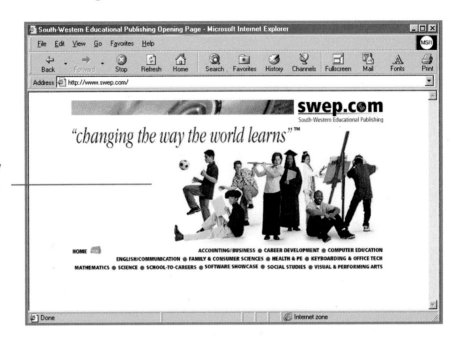

This Web page was created by the tags shown in Figure 1.1b. ———

Figure 1.1a
South-Western Educational Publishing Welcome page at *www.swep.com*

All of the words, pictures, and colors that you see in Figure 1.1a are organized and created by the HTML tags you see in the next figure, Figure 1.1b.

Figures 1.1a and 1.1b are actually the same page viewed in different ways.

```
swep.html - Notepad
File  Edit  Search  Help
<html>

<head>
<title>South-Western Educational Publishing Opening Page</title>
</head>
<script LANGUAGE="JavaScript">
<!-- hide script

Function preloadImages() {
    if (document.images) {
    if (typeof document.WM == 'undefined'){
        document.WM = new Object();
    }
        document.WM.loadedImages = new Array();
    var argLength = preloadImages.arguments.length;
    for(arg=0;arg<argLength;arg++) {
        document.WM.loadedImages[arg] = new Image();
        document.WM.loadedImages[arg].src = preloadImages.arguments[arg];
    }
  }
}

function pickgif(x,iname)
{
        var docname = "window.document." + iname;
        var fullname = "images/"+iname;
        var mainname = "images/";

        if (x) {
            fullname=fullname+"roll.gif";
            mainname=mainname+iname+"rollmain.gif";}
        else {
            fullname=fullname+".gif";
            mainname=mainname+"shoes.jpg";}
```

This page of HTML tags created the Web page shown in Figure 1.1a. ———

Figure 1.1b
HTML tags for the South-Western Educational Publishing Web page shown in Figure 1.1a

Chapter 1 Quick HTML Know-How

The World Wide Web (WWW) was created in the late 1980s in Europe. It was used limitedly in academic circles for about the next five years. However, it didn't capture the public's imagination until 1994 when a **Web browser** called **Mosaic** came on the scene. Mosaic was created at the University of Illinois. It was the first Web browser that allowed pictures and sound to accompany Web pages.

Internet Milestone

Business Discovers the Web

A new excitement was created around this new way to present and share information. Then, Netscape Communications Corporation released its browser called **Netscape Navigator**. Netscape caught the imagination of businesses in 1995, and everything was different from that point on.

In just a few short years, the World Wide Web became the new advertising and commercial medium that we see today. Billions and billions of dollars were invested by companies and corporations hoping to cash in on this new golden information sharing system. Suddenly, thousands and thousands of corporate **Webmasters** began to learn HTML so they could put their business Web pages online.

Figure 1.1b isn't very pretty. It shows the HTML tags that create the more exciting page shown in Figure 1.1a. Figure 1.1b shows exactly what the page behind the colorful page really looks like. The Web browser interprets the tags and creates the Web page the average Web surfer sees.

There are lots of tags and lots of ways to use them. This hint should help you from getting confused. *Remember that HTML tags are just instructions to the Web browser.* They tell the browser how to display information. Many times you can look at the final Web page and guess what the tags are that created the effect. If you remember this hint, learning HTML will be much easier.

Now it's your turn. Follow these steps to open a Web page you like. Viewing the page behind the page is as easy as selecting *Source* or some similar command from the *View* menu in your browser, as you can see in Figures 1.3a and 1.3b.

1. Open your Web browser by double-clicking on its icon, as shown in Figures 1.2a and 1.2b.

Figure 1.2a
Netscape Communicator icon

Figure 1.2b
Internet Explorer icon

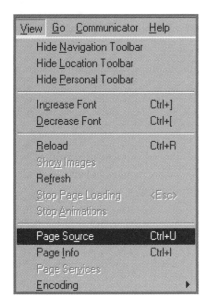

Figure 1.3a
The *View, Page Source* command in Netscape

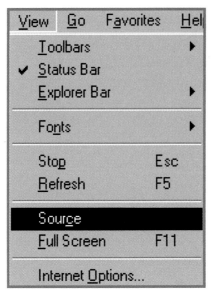

Figure 1.3b
The *View, Source* command in Internet Explorer

2 When a page appears, use your mouse to move your pointer over the *View* menu, as shown in Figures 1.3a and 1.3b.

3 Select *View* followed by *Source* in the Internet Explorer (IE) browser or *View* followed by either *Source, Page Source*, or *Document Source* in your version of the Netscape Navigator browser. (Note: Different browsers may use different words for this command. Look around; the option will be there.)

4 Examine the tags that appear on the page beneath the colorful page most people see. The tags will look something like the tags you saw in Figure 1.1b at the start of this lesson.

5 Jump around to three or four other Web pages and "View the Source." List seven tags that you keep running into over and over. Guess and record what they do in the table below.

Find Seven New Tags and Guess What They Do . . .

Number	Tag	The effect it causes on the Web page
Sample	⟨CENTER⟩⟨/CENTER⟩	*Centers text on a Web page.*
1.		
2.		
3.		
4.		
5.		
6.		
7.		

The World Wide Web is a large Web of computer networks that share HTML files. How many millions or billions of Web pages are there out in cyberspace? You could visit a new Web page every minute of every day for the rest of your life and never come close to reading a fraction of the available Web pages. While HTML has allowed people to share Web pages easily, has HTML also contributed to information overload?

NET FACT

Web Page, Home Page, Welcome Page, HTML Page . . . What's the Difference?

There are many terms used to describe HTML pages or documents. The truth is, these names are used so interchangeably that most people are totally unaware that there are slight distinctions in the meaning for the following terms:

- **Web page:** A Web page, or Web document, is any page created in HTML that can be placed on the World Wide Web.
- **Home page:** A home page is the main or primary Web page for a corporation, organization, or for an individual. Your home page is the first page you see as you start up your Web browser. When you click on the *Home* icon in your browser, you will go directly to your starting home page.
- **Welcome page:** A welcome page is designed especially for new visitors to a Web site.
- **HTML page:** An HTML page, or HTML document, is any document created in HTML that can be displayed on the World Wide Web.
- **Web site:** A Web site can include a collection of many interconnected Web pages organized by a specific company, organization, college or university, government agency, or by an individual. Web sites are stored on Web servers. There may be many Web sites and thousands of HTML pages on each Web site.

Is it all clear now? Don't let these subtle distinctions get in the way of your understanding of how the Web works. Underneath it all, you will still find HTML tags doing their job.

Enter Your Mystery Tags the Old Fashioned Way

There are many ways to create HTML Tags. You can use specialized software, such as FrontPage by Microsoft or Dreamweaver from Macromedia, to create super Web pages. With these programs, you can organize your HTML page, enter text, move things around, and create superior Web page effects without ever entering an HTML tag. You can do the same with many of the newer versions of word processing programs, such as Microsoft Word, WordPerfect, or WordPro. These word processors have HTML tags built right in.

You will want to use one of these kinds of programs for most of your Web pages. They are easy to use and give you lots of powerful HTML tools with which to work. However, for this activity, you are going to enter HTML tags the old fashioned way. And there are good reasons for doing this:

- First, by entering a few tags, you will develop a deeper understanding of how HTML really works.
- Second, you will be able to troubleshoot Web pages when picky little errors occur.
- Third, you will be able to view other pages and learn how they achieved certain effects.
- Fourth, you will understand a little better the file and folder structures found on Web computers.
- Finally, and most importantly, you will understand how HTML and JavaScript work together.

Learning to enter a few HTML tags in the old fashioned way will give you a big advantage as you start to learn JavaScript in Section 2. So, let's quickly cover the basics.

What To Use

Almost any word processing program or text editor will work for creating both HTML and JavaScript. This is one of the reasons HTML and JavaScript are so popular. You don't need any specialized software tools in order to create exciting Web pages like you need for Java, Shockwave, or some of the other software-intensive options.

Our recommendation is to use the simplest, most basic tools available:

- In Windows, you can use Notepad from the *Accessories* menu.
- On a Macintosh, you can use SimpleText.

These programs are easy to use and available on nearly every computer on the planet. You can also use your favorite word processing program, such as Microsoft Word, WordPerfect, WordPro, ClarisWorks, or even Microsoft Works. However, you will need to experiment a little bit with each word processing program to learn its

NET TIP

Uppercase or Lowercase

HTML is not case sensitive. You can use uppercase ⟨TAGS⟩, or you can use lowercase ⟨tags⟩. It really doesn't matter. However, each Web page designer has a preference. When asked, most HTML taggers will tell you that uppercase ⟨TAGS⟩ are easier to see. So, if you are emphasizing the tags, use uppercase ⟨TAGS⟩. But, if you would rather emphasize the words in the document, use lowercase ⟨tags⟩.

You can even mix uppercase ⟨TAGS⟩ and lowercase ⟨tags⟩ together, like this ⟨Tag⟩, or like this ⟨TAG⟩ ⟨/tag⟩. However, mixing cases is not considered good form. Do it if you like, but it's best to use all uppercase or all lowercase.

little idiosyncrasies. Instructions for Word and ClarisWorks are provided as examples. Most other word processors have similar features. Check the software's help system if you have any difficulties, or revert to Notepad or SimpleText to complete the activities.

Other more sophisticated programs, like FrontPage and Dreamweaver, really get the job done. Both provide options that allow you to see the tags. If you are using one of these two programs, click the *HTML Source* option so you can enter the tags directly.

In this activity, you will learn how to enter tags. In the next activity, you will learn to save your tags correctly. You will want to complete Activities 2 and 3 together; that is, back-to-back! Otherwise, you may have to enter everything twice, and that would be sad, indeed.

```
〈HTML〉
〈TITLE〉〈/TITLE〉
〈BODY〉
〈CENTER〉〈/CENTER〉
〈P〉〈/P〉
〈P〉〈/P〉
〈P〉〈/P〉
〈P〉〈/P〉
〈P〉〈/P〉
〈/BODY〉
〈/HTML〉
```

Figure 1.4
Enter these tags exactly as shown here.

1. Open Notepad, SimpleText, or your favorite word processing software.

2. Start a new document if necessary.

3. Enter the tags shown in Figure 1.4 in the exact order. Don't leave out an angle bracket 〈 or a slash /. Everything is important.

4. The tags you just entered are called the basic tags. They include a standard set of tags that appear in most Web pages. But your page will look very sad without some text. Enter the text between the tags, as shown in Figure 1.5. Notice that the new text to be entered is shown in bold.

```
〈HTML〉
〈TITLE〉HTML and JavaScript〈/TITLE〉
〈BODY〉
〈CENTER〉Creating HTML and JavaScript〈/CENTER〉
〈P〉Learning to create HTML tags can help you in many ways:〈/P〉
〈P〉You will develop a deeper understanding of how HTML really works.〈/P〉
〈P〉You will be able to troubleshoot Web pages when errors occur.〈/P〉
〈P〉You will be able to view other pages and learn how certain effects are created.〈/P〉
〈P〉You will understand how HTML and JavaScript work together.〈/P〉
〈/BODY〉
〈/HTML〉
```

Figure 1.5
Enter the text between the tags exactly as shown here.

5. Go on to Activity 1.3 now and learn how to save HTML pages so you won't have to enter all of this data again!! Hurry. Just stop long enough to read the *Thinking About Technology* information and go before the bell rings!

THINKING ABOUT TECHNOLOGY

What do you think the following tags will do on your page? Think about how these pairs of tags will make your page look. In the next *Thinking About Technology* segment, you will see what effect these tags will have.

〈HTML〉〈/HTML〉 _____

〈TITLE〉〈/TITLE〉 _____

〈BODY〉〈/BODY〉 _____

〈CENTER〉〈/CENTER〉 _____

〈P〉〈/P〉 _____

ACTIVITY

1.3

Objective:
In this activity, you will learn how to save your HTML document as a text file.

Save and View Your HTML Page

HTML documents are text files. This means that they are saved in the simplest way possible. For the most part, text files only save the letters you see on your keyboard. All of the sophisticated word processing commands are erased, leaving just the letters.

Saving as text allows HTML to move quickly over the Web. However, the problem with text files is that most people don't know how to save them. Before you save, there are a few things you need to know first.

File Types and File Extensions

To tell one kind of file from another, computers often add file extensions to file names. Sometimes you can see these extensions on your computer and sometimes you can't. Depending on your computer's settings, the extensions may or may not be visible, but the software on your computer knows the kinds of file types it can open.

Extensions are used a lot. For example, in Windows, text files are saved with a .txt ending or extension. If you use a word processor much, you may have seen these popular extensions:

.doc	Microsoft Word documents
.rtf	Microsoft's Rich Text Format
.wpd	Corel WordPerfect documents
.txt	text files
.html	HTML files
.htm	HTML files on some computer systems

HTML files are text files with an .html or an .htm extension. While the format you need for HTML is called text, the ending or extension must be .html (or .htm if you are using some older Windows-based software programs.) The *.html* extension signals to the Web browser that this is an HTML text file. The .html extension is like putting up a sign saying, "Hey browser, read me. I'm an HTML document."

Follow along. We are going to show you how to save with different software programs. Pick the software that most closely resembles the software on your computer system. They are:

- Notepad
- Microsoft Word
- SimpleText
- ClarisWorks for Macintosh

1 Select *Save As* from the *File* menu. (Word users beware! DO NOT select *Save As HTML* from the *File* menu if that option appears! Use the regular Save As command.)

2 From the *Save As* dialog box, create a *New Folder* in which to save your HTML and JavaScript work.

3 For both Notepad in Windows and SimpleText for Macintosh, the steps are very similar. (Note: Word processing users should skip to Step 4.)

a. Select the folder into which you wish to save your files.

b. Name your file as *One.html,* as shown in Figure 1.6. (Note: Older Windows systems will only accept a .htm extension.) Check with your teacher to make sure you saved your file properly. If everything saved okay, skip to Step 5.

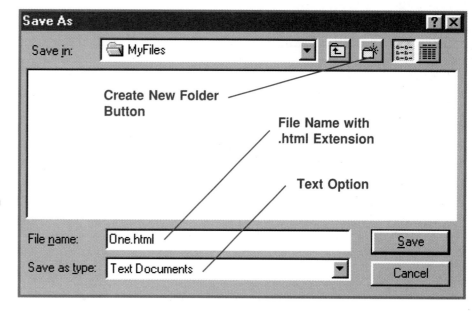

Figure 1.6
Naming text file with .html extension

4 In your word processing software, there are a few additional steps. While Notepad and SimpleText automatically save as text only, word processors save in their own unique format. You must select the proper text format from your saving options. Instructions for Word and Claris-Works are provided to help you learn this important step. Other word processors have text saving options. Check with your instructor to make sure you are following the steps properly for your software.

Microsoft Word for Windows 95, 98, or NT

a. Locate the folder in which you want to place your file.

b. Select *Text Only* as the *Save as type,* as shown in Figure 1.7.

c. Name your file *One.html.* (Note: In older Windows programs, the name will be truncated or shortened to *One.htm.*)

d. Click *Save.*

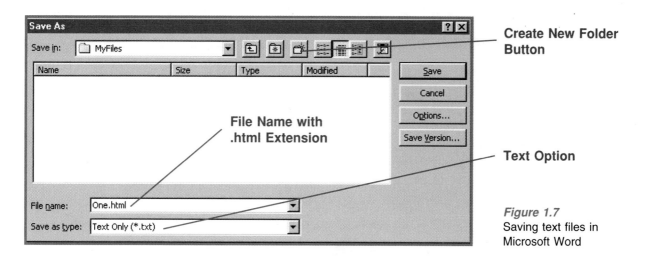

Figure 1.7
Saving text files in Microsoft Word

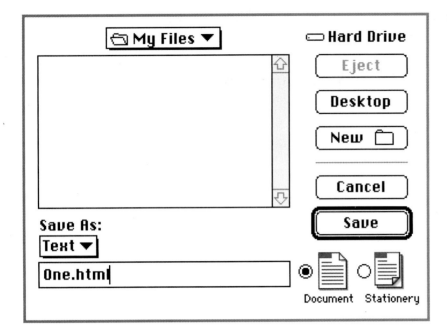

Figure 1.8
Saving text files in ClarisWorks

ClarisWorks for Macintosh

Macintosh computers make saving text files very easy.

a. Locate the folder into which you want to place your file.
b. Select *Text* as the *Save As* option.
c. Name your file *One.html,* as shown in Figure 1.8.
d. Click *Save.*

⑤ Viewing your HTML page in your Web browser is easy. There are a few minor browser variations, so we will give you several examples here to look at. We will show you how to do this in Windows and with Macintosh browsers.

Internet Explorer 4.0 in Windows 95, 98, NT or higher

a. Open your Web browser.
b. Click *File,* and then click *Open.*
c. Click on the *Browse* button to locate the folder in which you saved your file.
d. Select your HTML file, and click *Open.*
e. Click *OK,* as shown in Figure 1.9.

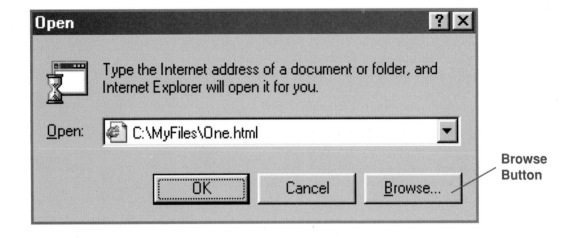

Figure 1.9
Find your file

Browse Button

Netscape 4.0 in Windows 95, 98, NT or higher

a. Open your Web browser.
b. Click *File,* and then click *Open Page.*
c. Click on the *Choose File* button to locate the folder in which you saved your file.

d. Select your HTML file, and click *Open.*
  e. Click *Open,* as shown in Figure 1.10.

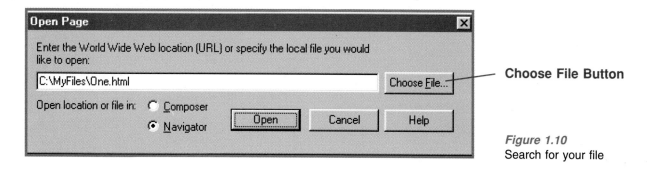

Choose File Button

Figure 1.10
Search for your file

Internet Explorer for Macintosh

  a. Open your Web browser.
  b. Click *File,* and then click *Open.*
  c. Browse to the Folder where you saved your file.
  d. Select your HTML file, and click *Open.*
  e. Click *Open,* as shown in Figure 1.11.

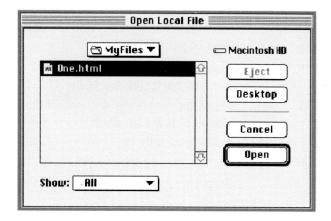

Figure 1.11
Find your file

Netscape for Macintosh

  a. Open your Web browser.
  b. Click *File,* and then click *Open File.*
  c. Browse to the Folder where you saved your file.
  d. Select your HTML file, and click *Open.*
  e. Click *Open,* as shown in Figure 1.12.

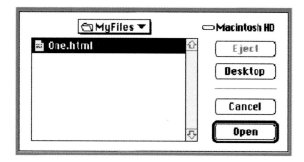

Figure 1.12
Find your file

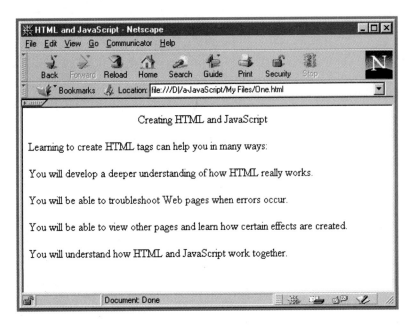

Creating HTML and JavaScript

Learning to create HTML tags can help you in many ways:

You will develop a deeper understanding of how HTML really works.

You will be able to troubleshoot Web pages when errors occur.

You will be able to view other pages and learn how certain effects are created.

You will understand how HTML and JavaScript work together.

6 View your file. It should look like Figure 1.13.

7 How does your Web page look? If you need to make corrections, make the corrections, save again, then return to your browser and look again at the changes you have made.

Figure 1.13
Congratulations! Your Web page probably looks like this sample!

THINKING ABOUT TECHNOLOGY

Here are the answers to the questions in the previous *Thinking About Technology* section.

⟨HTML⟩⟨/HTML⟩	Indicates the beginning and the end of an HTML Web page.
⟨TITLE⟩⟨/TITLE⟩	Places any text entered between these tags in the Title bar at the top of the Web page.
⟨BODY⟩⟨/BODY⟩	Marks the beginning and end of the text or information that will be displayed in the main portion of the Web browser window.
⟨CENTER⟩⟨/CENTER⟩	Centers text on the screen.
⟨P⟩⟨/P⟩	Puts a double space between text on the page.

Internet Milestone

The Browser Battles

In the last few years, Netscape's Navigator and Microsoft's **Internet Explorer** browsers have been fighting it out for supremacy in the Web browser world. This wasn't the first browser battle. In 1994, the dominant browser was called Mosaic. It was freeware out of the national supercomputing center at the University of Illinois in Champaign-Urbana. At the time Netscape came on the scene, Mosaic was adding 600,000 new users a month. But things changed in a hurry.

In the first three months of 1995, Netscape's Navigator browser gained a reputation for being a faster browser. By mid-year it had captured 50% of the browser users, and by the end of the year it commanded a whopping 80% of the browser market.

Netscape's dominance was quickly challenged by rival Microsoft who came out with its Internet Explorer browser. Microsoft gave away copies of its browser in hopes of cutting into Netscape's lead. Microsoft also had an advantage in that its Windows operating system ran on over 90% of personal computers. By making Windows and Internet Explorer work together, Microsoft created a more user-friendly Web system.

Microsoft's advantage, however, led to many legal battles. Several anti-trust lawsuits argued that Microsoft was using its dominance in Windows to crush Netscape and to eliminate its competition unfairly. Microsoft claimed it was simply adding more value for its customers by making its Internet Explorer browser easier to access.

The battle continues. Who will win in the end?

Using Headings

Most printed documents use headings to help the reader find important portions of text. Think of a report you have written for school. The main heading usually appears at the top and in the center of the page. Subheadings or secondary headings usually appear at the side of the paper. They are often shown in bold.

HTML gives you six standard headings or title sizes to choose from. In later activities, you will learn of more sophisticated ways to manipulate the size and appearance of text. Nevertheless, the heading tags will give you an easy way to control the size of your text, making it stand out so your reader can view the headings clearly.

The heading tags are easy to remember. They use a letter H with a number from 1 to 6 to indicate the level of the heading. Heading numbers indicate the level of importance for marked headings, with 1 being the most prominent and 6 being the least prominent. Look for:

⟨H1⟩⟨/H1⟩
⟨H2⟩⟨/H2⟩
⟨H3⟩⟨/H3⟩
⟨H4⟩⟨/H4⟩
⟨H5⟩⟨/H5⟩
⟨H6⟩⟨/H6⟩

Anything inside the heading tags will be made larger or smaller, depending on the number. For example:

⟨H1⟩VERY BIG⟨/H1⟩
⟨H3⟩In the Middle⟨/H3⟩
⟨H6⟩Very Small⟨/H6⟩

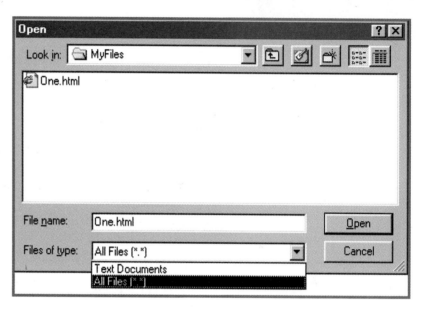

Figure 1.14a
Notepad users must select *All Files* in order to view their tags.

In this activity, you will open the HTML file you have been working on and add the heading or title tags.

1 Open your word processing software.

2 Re-open your *One.html* or *One.htm* file.

IMPORTANT NOTE to Notepad users: Select *All Files* under the *Files of type* option, as shown in Figure 1.14a. Otherwise, you will not be able to view your .html or .htm file!

IMPORTANT NOTE to Microsoft Word users: When you open an .html file, Word may display your Web page as it would appear in a Web browser. In order to view the HTML tags, select *HTML Source* from the *View* menu, as shown in Figure 1.14b, and you can continue to work on your tags.

Figure 1.14b
Microsoft Word users must select *HTML Source* in order to view their tags.

3 Enter the heading tags shown in Figure 1.15.

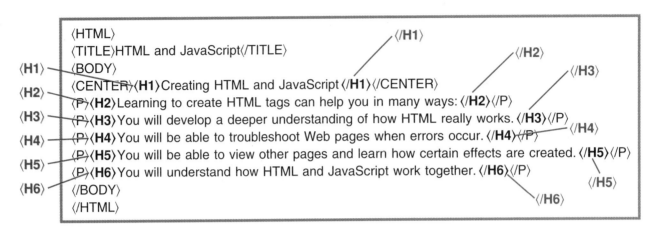

```
⟨HTML⟩
⟨TITLE⟩HTML and JavaScript⟨/TITLE⟩
⟨BODY⟩
⟨CENTER⟩⟨H1⟩Creating HTML and JavaScript ⟨/H1⟩⟨/CENTER⟩
⟨P⟩⟨H2⟩Learning to create HTML tags can help you in many ways: ⟨/H2⟩⟨/P⟩
⟨P⟩⟨H3⟩You will develop a deeper understanding of how HTML really works. ⟨/H3⟩⟨/P⟩
⟨P⟩⟨H4⟩You will be able to troubleshoot Web pages when errors occur. ⟨/H4⟩⟨/P⟩
⟨P⟩⟨H5⟩You will be able to view other pages and learn how certain effects are created. ⟨/H5⟩⟨/P⟩
⟨P⟩⟨H6⟩You will understand how HTML and JavaScript work together. ⟨/H6⟩⟨/P⟩
⟨/BODY⟩
⟨/HTML⟩
```

Figure 1.15
Add the heading tags

4 Save your new HTML page as *Two.html* or *Two.htm*.

5 Open your Web browser, open the *Two.html* file, and view it. It should look like Figure 1.16.

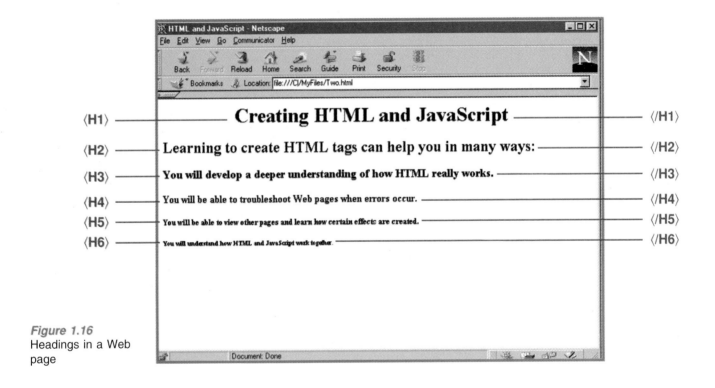

Figure 1.16
Headings in a Web page

Heading ⟨H⟩⟨/H⟩ tags really change the look of a page. In our example in Figure 1.16, however, the heading tags are misused. At best, there are only three levels of the document information:

⟨H1⟩   The title at the top
⟨H2⟩   The introductory line followed by a colon (:)
⟨H3⟩   The list of four reasons to learn HTML tags

Return to your document and reorganize the heading tags. Use no more than three ⟨H⟩⟨/H⟩ tags. Think about it for a second, then make your document comfortable to read, emphasizing the three levels this document dictates.

IMPORTANT NOTE to Notepad users: Remember to select *All Files* under the *Files As Type* option, as shown in Figure 1.14a. Otherwise, you will not be able to view your .html or .htm file!

IMPORTANT NOTE to Microsoft Word users: Remember that when you open an .html file, Word may display your Web page as it would appear in a Web browser. In order to view the HTML tags, select *HTML Source* from the *View* menu, as shown in Figure 1.14b, and you can continue to work on your tags.

Net Fun

Do you want to visit an exciting place? Try Excite at *www.excite.com*. Excite is one of the most popular Web searching systems. With Excite, you can look up anything on everything. Try entering the search words *HTML* or *JavaScript* in the search window and see what you get.

ACTIVITY

1.5

Objective:

In this activity, you will create ordered and numbered lists.

Numbered and Bulleted Lists

In the last *Thinking About Technology* section, you were asked to reorganize your *Two.html* file and use the ⟨H⟩ tags in a more consistent manner. In this activity, we are going to whip things into shape even further.

One of the most powerful ways to organize information on a Web page is by the use of lists. There are several kinds of lists, including the following:

Unordered (usually bulleted) lists   ⟨UL⟩⟨/UL⟩
Ordered or numbered lists   ⟨OL⟩⟨/OL⟩

The unordered list tags ⟨UL⟩⟨/UL⟩ will create a bulleted list. Start your list with the opening ⟨UL⟩ unordered list tag, mark the items to be listed with the list ⟨LI⟩⟨/LI⟩ tag, and place a ⟨/UL⟩ tag at the end of your list. Try it!

Creating an Unordered List

Unordered lists are used whenever the items in the list can appear in any order. Here is how to create an unordered list in HTML:

1 Open your *Two.html* file.

IMPORTANT NOTE to Notepad users: Remember to select *All Files* under the *Files As Type* option, as shown in Figure 1.14a. Otherwise, you will not be able to view your .html or .htm file!

NOTE to Microsoft Word users: Remember that when you open an .html file, Word may display your Web page as it would appear in a Web browser. In order to view the HTML tags, select *HTML Source* from the *View* menu, as shown in Figure 1.14b, and you can continue to work on your tags.

2 Enter the ⟨UL⟩⟨/UL⟩ tags at the start and at the end of the list, as shown in Figure 1.17.

3 Add the ⟨LI⟩⟨/LI⟩ tags for each sentence in the list, as shown in Figure 1.17.

4 Save your file as *Three.html.*

5 View your page to see how it looks. It should be similar to Figure 1.18.

Creating an Ordered List

Ordered lists are used whenever the items should appear in a specific order or if you are counting items in a list. This list gives four reasons to learn HTML tags. Let's quickly convert it to an ordered or numbered list:

6 Open your *Three.html* file.

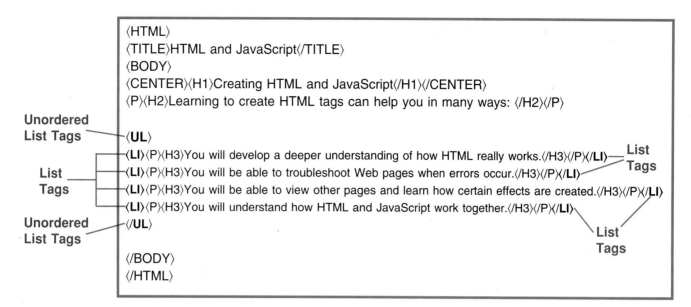

⟨HTML⟩
⟨TITLE⟩HTML and JavaScript⟨/TITLE⟩
⟨BODY⟩
⟨CENTER⟩⟨H1⟩Creating HTML and JavaScript⟨/H1⟩⟨/CENTER⟩
⟨P⟩⟨H2⟩Learning to create HTML tags can help you in many ways: ⟨/H2⟩⟨/P⟩

Unordered List Tags ⟨UL⟩

List Tags
⟨**LI**⟩⟨P⟩⟨H3⟩You will develop a deeper understanding of how HTML really works.⟨/H3⟩⟨/P⟩⟨**/LI**⟩ **List Tags**
⟨**LI**⟩⟨P⟩⟨H3⟩You will be able to troubleshoot Web pages when errors occur.⟨/H3⟩⟨/P⟩⟨**/LI**⟩
⟨**LI**⟩⟨P⟩⟨H3⟩You will be able to view other pages and learn how certain effects are created.⟨/H3⟩⟨/P⟩⟨**/LI**⟩
⟨**LI**⟩⟨P⟩⟨H3⟩You will understand how HTML and JavaScript work together.⟨/H3⟩⟨/P⟩⟨**/LI**⟩

Unordered List Tags ⟨**/UL**⟩
List Tags

⟨/BODY⟩
⟨/HTML⟩

Figure 1.17
Enter the Unordered list tags

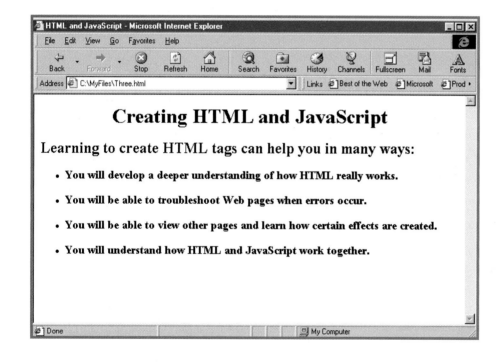

Figure 1.18
An unordered list

IMPORTANT NOTE to Notepad users: Remember to select *All Files* under the *Files As Type* option, as shown in Figure 1.14a. Otherwise, you will not be able to view your .html or .htm file!

NOTE to Microsoft Word users: Remember that when you open an .html file, Word may display your Web page as it would appear in a Web browser. In order to view the HTML tags, select *HTML Source* from the *View* menu, as shown in Figure 1.14b, and you can continue to work on your tags.

7 Change the pair of ⟨UL⟩⟨/UL⟩ tags to ⟨OL⟩⟨/OL⟩ tags, as shown in Figure 1.19. No other changes are necessary. (Note: Don't use a zero; use the letter O for ordered.)

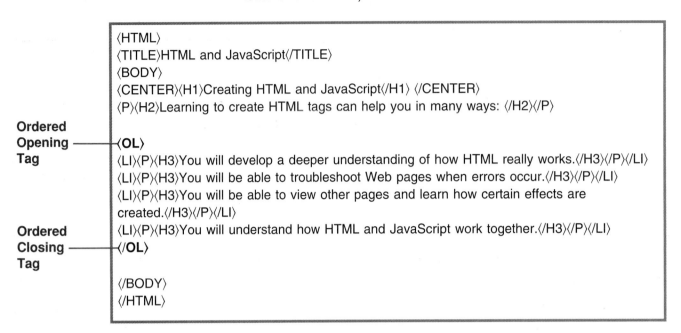

⟨HTML⟩
⟨TITLE⟩HTML and JavaScript⟨/TITLE⟩
⟨BODY⟩
⟨CENTER⟩⟨H1⟩Creating HTML and JavaScript⟨/H1⟩ ⟨/CENTER⟩
⟨P⟩⟨H2⟩Learning to create HTML tags can help you in many ways: ⟨/H2⟩⟨/P⟩

Ordered Opening Tag — ⟨OL⟩
⟨LI⟩⟨P⟩⟨H3⟩You will develop a deeper understanding of how HTML really works.⟨/H3⟩⟨/P⟩⟨/LI⟩
⟨LI⟩⟨P⟩⟨H3⟩You will be able to troubleshoot Web pages when errors occur.⟨/H3⟩⟨/P⟩⟨/LI⟩
⟨LI⟩⟨P⟩⟨H3⟩You will be able to view other pages and learn how certain effects are created.⟨/H3⟩⟨/P⟩⟨/LI⟩
⟨LI⟩⟨P⟩⟨H3⟩You will understand how HTML and JavaScript work together.⟨/H3⟩⟨/P⟩⟨/LI⟩
Ordered Closing Tag — ⟨/OL⟩

⟨/BODY⟩
⟨/HTML⟩

Figure 1.19
Enter the Ordered list tags

8 Save your file as *Four.html*.

9 View your page to see how it looks. It should look similar to Figure 1.20.

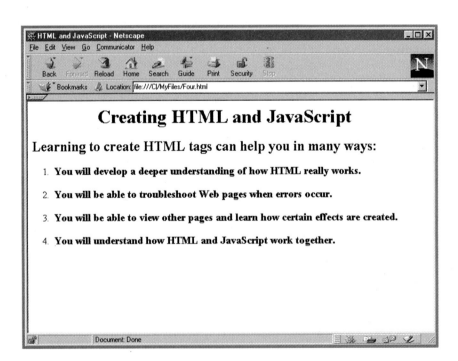

Figure 1.20
An ordered or numbered list

Embedding and Indenting Lists

Sometimes you may want to have a list inside a list, as you would in an outline. In this set of steps, you will indent and create unordered lists inside the numbered list.

10 Open your *Four.html* file.

11 Add two pairs of ⟨UL⟩⟨/UL⟩ tags in the middle of the list, as shown in Figure 1.21.

⟨HTML⟩
⟨TITLE⟩HTML and JavaScript⟨/TITLE⟩
⟨BODY⟩
⟨CENTER⟩⟨H1⟩Creating HTML and JavaScript⟨/H1⟩⟨/CENTER⟩
⟨P⟩⟨H2⟩Learning to create HTML tags can help you in many ways: ⟨/H2⟩⟨/P⟩

⟨OL⟩
⟨LI⟩⟨P⟩⟨H3⟩You will develop a deeper understanding of how HTML really works.⟨/H3⟩⟨/P⟩⟨/LI⟩

Unordered Opening Tag → **⟨UL⟩**

⟨LI⟩⟨P⟩⟨H3⟩You will be able to troubleshoot Web pages when errors occur.⟨/H3⟩⟨/P⟩⟨/LI⟩
⟨UL⟩
⟨LI⟩⟨P⟩⟨H3⟩You will be able to view other pages and learn how certain effects are created.⟨/H3⟩⟨/P⟩⟨/LI⟩

Unordered Closing Tag → **⟨/UL⟩**
⟨/UL⟩

⟨LI⟩⟨P⟩⟨H3⟩You will understand how HTML and JavaScript work together.⟨/H3⟩⟨/P⟩⟨/LI⟩
⟨/OL⟩
⟨/BODY⟩
⟨/HTML⟩

Figure 1.21
Enter the unordered list tags

The Life of a Webmaster

A Webmaster is the person assigned to maintain Web pages for a Web site. The job of a Webmaster has grown and expanded. Not only do Webmasters need to know how to create Web pages, but they need to know how to write clearly, use artwork effectively, and create links from one page to another. They also must help others post their documents on the Web in an attractive and readable way. Webmasters often work long hours, updating pages late into the night when other people are home watching reruns of Seinfeld.

Some of the best ways to prepare for a Webmaster job would be to take every Computer Education, Language Arts, and Art class that your school offers.

12 Save your file as *Five.html*.

13 View your page to see how it looks. It should look similar to Figure 1.22.

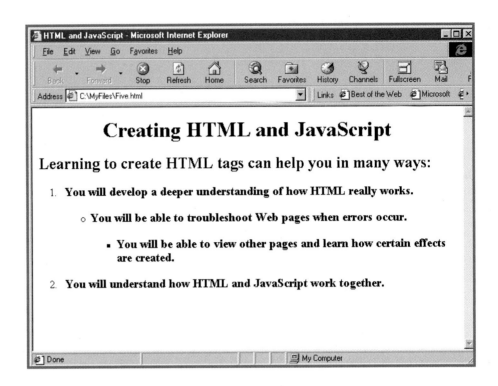

Figure 1.22
Embedded and indented lists

How can you create a sophisticated outline in HTML? You know, the kind you had to do for your last research paper? Can you see yourself doing your next research paper online in HTML? Find the error in the following list:

```
⟨OL⟩
⟨LI⟩Item A
  ⟨UL⟩
  ⟨LI⟩Item A1
  ⟨LI⟩Item A2
  ⟨/UL⟩
⟨LI⟩Item B
  ⟨UL⟩
  ⟨LI⟩Item B1
  ⟨LI⟩Item B2
  ⟨/UL⟩
⟨/UL⟩
```

NET VOCABULARY

Define the following terms:

1. angle brackets
2. home page
3. HTML
4. HTML page
5. Hypertext Markup Language
6. Internet Explorer

7. Java
8. JavaScript
9. Mosaic
10. Netscape Navigator
11. VRML
12. Web browser

13. Web page
14. Web site
15. Webmasters
16. welcome page

NET REVIEW

Give a short answer to the following questions:

1. Think of a way to explain how HTML tags work to people who have never created a Web page before in their lives. How can you explain how HTML works to a novice?

2. Explain the process of viewing the HTML source code for an HTML Web page.

3. Explain how you must save HTML text pages.

4. What are file name extensions? Give examples.

_____

_____

_____

_____

5. What are Mosaic, Netscape Navigator/Communicator, and Internet Explorer? What has each contributed to the growth of the Web?

_____

_____

_____

_____

FINDING ONLINE HTML RESOURCES

You have just been hired as the Webmaster for Great Applications, Inc., but your HTML skills are limited. You need to find some good HTML information fast! What do you do?

The answer is obvious. Hit the Web. Pick a search engine, such as Yahoo!, Excite, Lycos, or some other search tool, and enter these search words:

- Hypertext Markup Language
- HTML
- HTML Guides
- Learning HTML

Record the title and URL or Web address, and write a brief summary of the helpful HTML Web pages you find in the table below:

Title that Appears in the Title Bar	Web Address or URL	Description

NET PROJECT TEAMWORK   The Seven Greatest Web Pages on the Net

Great Applications, Inc. is looking for design ideas for their new Web site welcome page. In a team of three or four, create a list of your favorite Web pages. Find seven great Web pages and discuss what makes them so cool. Vote, and make your vote count as you rank the seven welcome pages from Number 1 to Number 7. List your team's choices here for future reference.

Ranking	Title as It Appears in the Title Bar	Web Address or URL

Web sites are important for many companies, groups, and individuals. We all know that many businesses would go out of business without a quality Web site. But just how important is a great-looking Web site for non-commercial organizations and government agencies?
List reasons why these organizations need Web sites.

Government agencies:

_____

_____

_____

_____

Non-profit organizations:

_____

_____

_____

Universities:

_____

_____

_____

HTML Organization Techniques

Chapter Objectives

In this chapter, you will discover how to organize your Web page. After reading Chapter 2, you will be able to

1 organize page information with single and double spacing.

2 organize page information with lines.

3 implement attributes and values.

4 change Web page color defaults by altering attributes and values.

5 alter the text colors.

6 create three types of hyperlinks:
- Links to another spot within your own document.
- Links to a URL or Web page anywhere on the WWW.
- Links to another Web page on your own computer.

HTML Terms

attributes

fonts

hexadecimal

HTTP

hyperlinks

hypertext links

Hypertext Transfer Protocol

values

Creating Better Web Pages

The World Wide Web is a creation of hundreds of thousands of people who are constantly creating, improving, and posting exciting Web pages. The Web is a place to be totally creative. All you need to know to join in the fun is a little knowledge of HTML and JavaScript. With these tools in your bag of tricks, you will be limited only by your own imagination.

As you have surfed the Web, you have seen wonderfully exciting Web pages, and you have seen other pages that fall flat. The main difference between a great page and a dull page comes down to the little things—the choice of fonts, colors, pictures, and the selection of elements that help with the overall organization of your pages.

There are many HTML techniques you can use to make your pages perfectly presentable. There are single- and double-spacing techniques, line techniques, and other specialized organizing tags that can make any Web page easy to read. For example, Web pages can be made more appealing by adding white space between paragraphs or by placing lines between different sections of a Web page. Changing the colors of your text and page background can also make an HTML document more appealing. Color choices are extremely important. There is nothing uglier in cyberspace than a Web page that mixes all the wrong colors. Use just the right colors, and your page will be fabulous.

Fonts, or the style of letters, can be altered. Every font has a style all its own. Here are some samples of the most common fonts.

- This is Times New Roman.
- **This is Arial.**
- `This is Courier.`

Hypertext links help to make Web pages interesting and easy to navigate. **Hyperlinks** allow users to click and zoom off to another place in cyberspace, to another page they have created, or to a spot within the current document. If you have a lot of information on a single page, creating an index can help your reader hyper-jump to the exact information for which they are looking.

As you learn the new HTML elements taught in this chapter, new ideas on how to organize your Web pages will come to you. ■

Net Fun

Want to drive someone crazy? Use the Blink tag. Put the tags ⟨BLINK⟩⟨/BLINK⟩ around any group of words and they will blink on and off like the neon lights on a third-rate casino in Atlantic City. The blink tag will drive your Web page viewers to distraction.

Single and Double Spacing

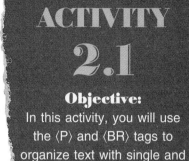

Most early Web pages, before 1995, are best-described as long, boring, collections of words. Early versions of HTML supplied only the simplest ways to break up text into readable sections.

That has changed. There is no longer any reason to create a boring, hard to read Web page. In this activity, you will see first-hand how to improve the readability and organization of your page.

1. Open your word processing software.

2. Enter the following Web page information exactly as you see it.

Note for Notepad users: Select the *Word Wrap* option from the *Edit* menu before you enter the text.

```
⟨HTML⟩
⟨TITLE⟩HTML and JavaScript⟨/TITLE⟩

⟨BODY⟩
⟨CENTER⟩⟨H1⟩Organizing Tags⟨/H1⟩⟨/CENTER⟩

There are many ways to organize a Web page. This Web page will
organize text, hypertext links, colors, and fonts. It will also
demonstrate single spacing, double spacing, and the use of line
breaks.

This Web page will display how to organize Web pages in a number
of ways using:

Powerful Lines
Hyperlinks to HTML and JavaScript Sources
Hyperlinks to Previously Created Web Pages
Fancy Fonts
Perfect Pictures
Orderly Tables
Extraordinary Extras

⟨/BODY⟩
⟨/HTML⟩
```

Figure 2.1
Enter these tags and words exactly as shown.

3. Save the file as you learned to save in Activity 1.3 with the name *Six.html* or *Six.htm.*

④ Open your Web browser and view your page. It should look messy, as seen in Figure 2.2.

(Refer back to Activity 1.3 if you need a reminder on how to view an .html file in your Web browser.)

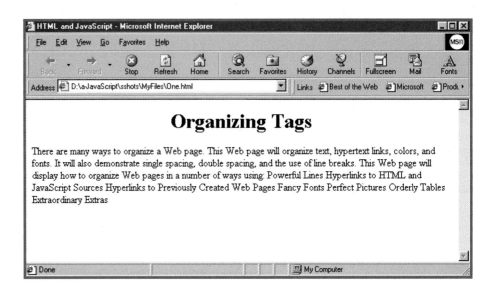

Figure 2.2
An unorganized Web page

Notice that while the page may look organized when you entered it in HTML, the organization of the page "falls apart" on the Web without a few organizing tags. The use of a few selected tags can really clean up a page.

The two easiest tags to use to organize a page are the ⟨P⟩⟨/P⟩, or paragraph tags, and the ⟨BR⟩, or break tag.

- The ⟨P⟩⟨/P⟩ tags create a double space around the text.
- The ⟨BR⟩ tag creates a single-spaced break.

⑤ Reopen your *Six.html* file in your word processor.

Note for Notepad users: Select the *Word Wrap* option from the *Edit* menu when you open the file so that you can see all of the text on your screen.

⑥ Add the ⟨P⟩⟨/P⟩ and ⟨BR⟩⟨/BR⟩ tags, as marked in bold in Figure 2.3.

⑦ Use the *Save As* option to save your reorganized file as *Seven.html* or *Seven.htm*.

⑧ Review your work. It should look much better this time, as shown in Figure 2.4.

THINKING ABOUT TECHNOLOGY

White space is important for the readers of a document. White space is a term used to describe the area around text that allows the user's eye to rest and find important parts of a document. White space helps open up

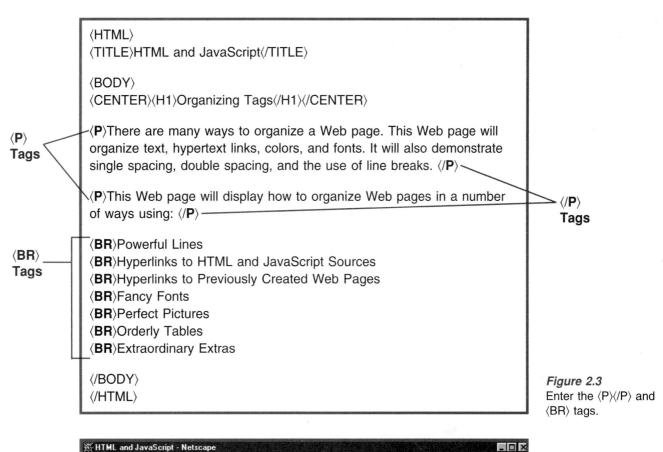

⟨P⟩ Tags

⟨BR⟩ Tags

```
⟨HTML⟩
⟨TITLE⟩HTML and JavaScript⟨/TITLE⟩

⟨BODY⟩
⟨CENTER⟩⟨H1⟩Organizing Tags⟨/H1⟩⟨/CENTER⟩

⟨P⟩There are many ways to organize a Web page. This Web page will
organize text, hypertext links, colors, and fonts. It will also demonstrate
single spacing, double spacing, and the use of line breaks. ⟨/P⟩

⟨P⟩This Web page will display how to organize Web pages in a number
of ways using: ⟨/P⟩

⟨BR⟩Powerful Lines
⟨BR⟩Hyperlinks to HTML and JavaScript Sources
⟨BR⟩Hyperlinks to Previously Created Web Pages
⟨BR⟩Fancy Fonts
⟨BR⟩Perfect Pictures
⟨BR⟩Orderly Tables
⟨BR⟩Extraordinary Extras

⟨/BODY⟩
⟨/HTML⟩
```

⟨/P⟩ Tags

Figure 2.3
Enter the ⟨P⟩⟨/P⟩ and
⟨BR⟩ tags.

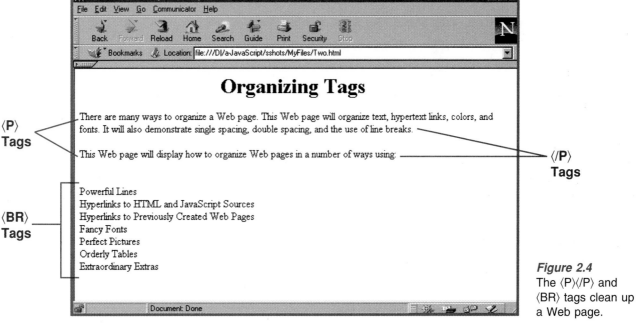

⟨P⟩ Tags

⟨BR⟩ Tags

⟨/P⟩ Tags

Figure 2.4
The ⟨P⟩⟨/P⟩ and
⟨BR⟩ tags clean up
a Web page.

THINKING ABOUT TECHNOLOGY (continued)

a document to the human eye. Compare Figures 2.2 and 2.4 to see what
we mean by the lack of white space. Figure 2.2 looks terrible. There is
no white space breaking up the words in the text. In Figure 2.4, the problem has been corrected. The document is much easier to read. How
does white space make a document easier to read?

ACTIVITY

2.2

Objective:
In this activity, you will learn to change the background color of your Web page, and you will create lines of varying width and length using attributes and values.

Lines and Background Colors

Attributes and Values

HTML tags can be enhanced by giving them **attributes** and **values**. Take the ⟨BODY⟩ tag. You can add elements to the body tag that will dramatically change the look of your Web page. For example, to change the background color of your Web page, you can add the background attribute command and give the tag a color value, as shown in Figure 2.5.

Try it!

1 Open your *Seven.html* file.

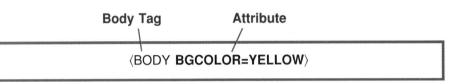

Figure 2.5
Changing background colors

Reminder for Notepad users: Don't forget to select the *Word Wrap* option from the *Edit* menu when you open the file.

2 Enter BGCOLOR=YELLOW inside the BODY tag near the top of your Web page, as shown in bold in Figure 2.5.

3 Save your work as *Eight.html*.

4 View these changes in your Web browser. Your page should turn yellow.

5 Experiment. Change the attribute to BLUE, GREEN, RED, WHITE, or another color of your choice.

NET FACT

Hexadecimal Colors

Computers speak only in numbers. Values are expressed as numbers that the computer understands. Color values can be carefully controlled and changed to match virtually every color in the rainbow by using the hexadecimal values for certain colors.

Hexadecimal digits operate on a base-16 number system rather than the base-10 number system we humans normally use. Hexadecimal numbers use the letters A, B, C, D, E, and F along with the numbers 0 to 9 to create their 16 different digits.

For example, look at the following color values expressed as numbers:

White	= #FFFFFF	Green	= #00FF00
Black	= #000000	Blue	= #0000FF
Red	= #FF0000	Yellow	= #FFFF00

Shades of these colors are created by changing the numbers. For example, a really great sky blue can be created on your HTML page with the number 00CCFF. Do you want a nice light purple? Try FF95FF. An ugly slime green can be created with AAFF00.

Substitute text color values with numbers in your Web page and see what happens. For example, try this:

BGCOLOR=#AAFF00 VLINK=#FF95FF TEXT=#00CCFF LINK=#FFFF00

Attributes and values are powerful tools to help you organize your Web pages. One of the most widely used tags is the ⟨HR⟩, or Horizontal Rule. With your *Eight.html* file open, add the set of tags shown in Figure 2.6. The first ⟨HR⟩ tag marked in Figure 2.6 doesn't use attributes or values. The tag simply creates a horizontal line across the page. The other three ⟨HR⟩ tags use attributes and values to change the shape and size of the lines.

6 Reopen your *Eight.html* file. Enter the various ⟨HR⟩ tags, attributes and values as marked in bold near the end of Figure 2.6 near the bottom of the page before the ⟨/BODY⟩ tag.

Figure 2.6
Adding background colors and lines

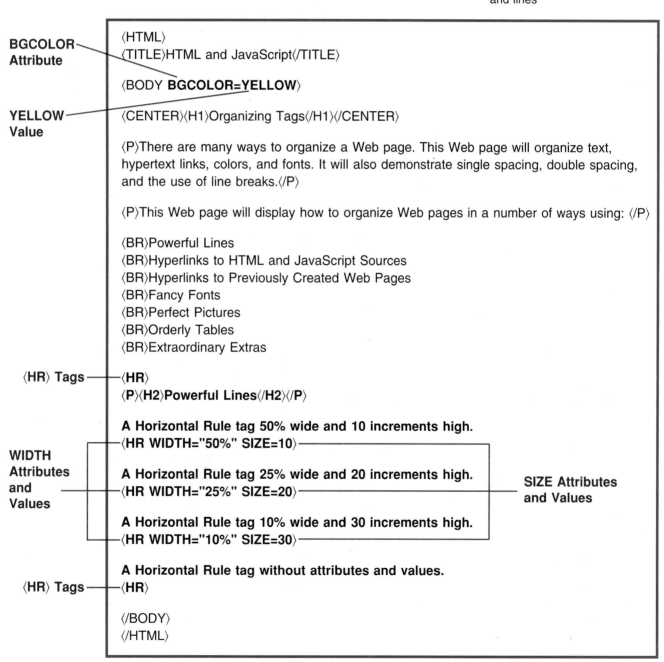

BGCOLOR
Attribute

YELLOW
Value

⟨HR⟩ Tags

WIDTH
Attributes
and
Values

SIZE Attributes
and Values

⟨HR⟩ Tags

```
⟨HTML⟩
⟨TITLE⟩HTML and JavaScript⟨/TITLE⟩

⟨BODY BGCOLOR=YELLOW⟩

⟨CENTER⟩⟨H1⟩Organizing Tags⟨/H1⟩⟨/CENTER⟩

⟨P⟩There are many ways to organize a Web page. This Web page will organize text,
hypertext links, colors, and fonts. It will also demonstrate single spacing, double spacing,
and the use of line breaks.⟨/P⟩

⟨P⟩This Web page will display how to organize Web pages in a number of ways using: ⟨/P⟩

⟨BR⟩Powerful Lines
⟨BR⟩Hyperlinks to HTML and JavaScript Sources
⟨BR⟩Hyperlinks to Previously Created Web Pages
⟨BR⟩Fancy Fonts
⟨BR⟩Perfect Pictures
⟨BR⟩Orderly Tables
⟨BR⟩Extraordinary Extras

⟨HR⟩
⟨P⟩⟨H2⟩Powerful Lines⟨/H2⟩⟨/P⟩

A Horizontal Rule tag 50% wide and 10 increments high.
⟨HR WIDTH="50%" SIZE=10⟩

A Horizontal Rule tag 25% wide and 20 increments high.
⟨HR WIDTH="25%" SIZE=20⟩

A Horizontal Rule tag 10% wide and 30 increments high.
⟨HR WIDTH="10%" SIZE=30⟩

A Horizontal Rule tag without attributes and values.
⟨HR⟩

⟨/BODY⟩
⟨/HTML⟩
```

7 Save your file as *Nine.html*.

8 View the horizontal lines in your Web browser. The page should look like Figure 2.7.

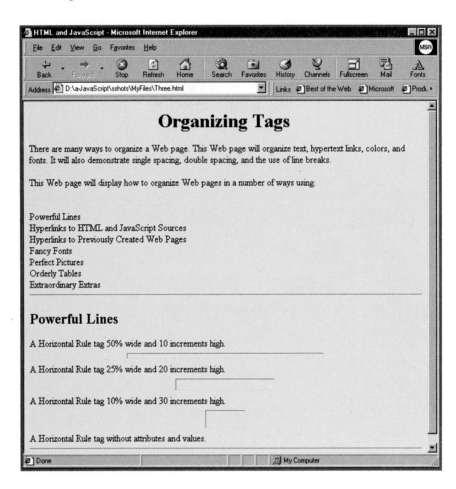

Figure 2.7
Powerful lines

THINKING ABOUT TECHNOLOGY

How can you use lines and colors to jazz up your pages? When is it appropriate to use a full 100% line? When is it better to use a half or 50% line or even a smaller 25% line? How wide can you make lines appear?

Bad Color Choices

It is considered impolite to display a Web page that is hard to read. Some Web page builders select backgrounds and colors that make their Web pages hard to read. Before you post your Web page to the WWW, test your pages and make sure all of the text appears clearly on the page and that your color choices don't detract from what you are trying to say.

Also, it is a good idea to think about the visually impaired and those who may suffer from color blindness when making your color selections. Mixing red and green color shades in an incorrect way can cause colorblind people to struggle with the text. Making your font sizes too small can cause trouble for those who have a hard time seeing. Having a dark background and dark letters can make a page difficult for anyone to read.

Hyperlinks Inside Your Document

Web pages became popular because they could link easily to other pages, or to various sections inside a document at the speed of an electron. Hyperlinks are easy to use, but a little more difficult to understand at first.

To use a hyperlink, you just click on the link. Links may be pictures or words that are underlined and appear in a different color, as shown in Figure 2.8.

Hyperlinks are created with special tags called anchor tags. The tag has several parts. The opening and closing tags are called the anchor or link tags and look like this:

⟨A HREF="*insert location of file*"⟩⟨/A⟩

Link or anchor tags are fairly useless unless you define a place to which you are linking. There are several ways to use link tags. You can:

- Link to another spot within your own document.
- Link to a URL or Web page anywhere on the WWW.
- Link to another Web page on your own computer.

In Activity 2.4 you will link to the WWW, and in Activity 2.5 you will create hyperlinks to all the Web pages you have created so far. In this activity, we will start linking within your HTML page.

ACTIVITY
2.3

Objective:
In this activity, you will learn to create hypertext links inside your document using anchor tags.

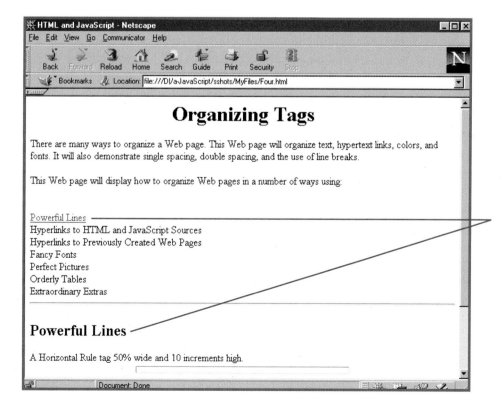

This link will jump down to here when you click on it.

Figure 2.8
A hypertext link

These internal hyperlinks help users navigate between important parts of your Web page.

The first ⟨A⟩ tag you insert will create a hypertext link to a location within your document. You will create the tag in Step 2. The attribute is HREF= and the value is "#POWERFUL." The quotation marks are necessary, as is the # or pound sign.

The second anchor tag will identify the exact location in your Web page to which you want to link. In Step 4, you will create a tag with the attribute NAME= and a value called "POWERFUL."

1 Open your *Nine.html* file.

2 Change the background color back to white by changing the BGCOLOR attribute from YELLOW to **WHITE**.

3 Add the following anchor ⟨**A**⟩⟨**/A**⟩ tags before and after the first *Powerful Lines* list item, as shown here and in Figure 2.9. (Note: The pound sign # can be created by holding the Shift key down and pressing the number 3. The double quote marks " are created by holding down shift and pressing the single quote ' character.)

⟨BR⟩ ⟨**A HREF="#POWERFUL"**⟩Powerful Lines⟨**/A**⟩

4 Insert the following anchor ⟨**A**⟩⟨**/A**⟩ tags around the second *Powerful Lines* list item, as shown here and marked in bold in Figure 2.9.

⟨P⟩⟨H2⟩⟨**A NAME= "POWERFUL"**⟩Powerful Lines⟨**/A**⟩⟨/H2⟩⟨/P⟩

5 Save your new file as *Ten.html*.

6 View the changes in your Web browser. Your link should look like the sample in Figure 2.8. When you click the link, you should jump down the page to the Powerful Lines heading in your document.

Net Ethics   RESPECT the WWW

What you write in a Web page shouldn't be offensive to others. You are responsible for what you create and post on the WWW. RESPECT the Web. When creating your Web pages, consider these guidelines:

R = *Responsibility*: Assume personal responsibility, and create only ethical and appropriate pages.

E = *Everybody*: Try to create Web pages that everybody will enjoy, appreciate, and consider of value.

S = *Simplicity*: Make your Web pages easy to navigate. Make information simple to find.

P = *Purpose*: Have a clear purpose for every Web page you put on the Web. Don't post unnecessary pages.

E = *Ethical*: Make sure all the content of every Web page you post corresponds to your values and has a beneficial purpose.

C = *Correct*: Make sure all the words on your page are spelled correctly, all the sentences are written correctly, and that all the hyperlinks work.

T = *Totally worth visiting*: Try to create pages that others will think are totally worth someone's time to visit.

```
〈HTML〉
〈TITLE〉HTML and JavaScript〈/TITLE〉

〈BODY BGCOLOR=WHITE〉
〈CENTER〉〈H1〉Organizing Tags〈/H1〉〈/CENTER〉

〈P〉There are many ways to organize a Web page. This Web page will organize text, hypertext links, colors,
and fonts. It will also demonstrate single spacing, double spacing, and the use of line breaks.〈/P〉

〈P〉This Web page will display how to organize Web pages in a number of ways using: 〈/P〉

〈BR〉〈A HREF="#POWERFUL"〉Powerful Lines〈/A〉
〈BR〉Hyperlinks to HTML and JavaScript Sources
〈BR〉Hyperlinks to Previously Created Web Pages
〈BR〉Fancy Fonts
〈BR〉Perfect Pictures
〈BR〉Orderly Tables
〈BR〉Extraordinary Extras

〈HR〉
〈P〉〈H2〉〈A NAME="POWERFUL"〉Powerful Lines〈/A〉〈/H2〉〈/P〉

A Horizontal Rule tag 50% wide and 10 increments high.
〈HR WIDTH="50%" SIZE=10〉

A Horizontal Rule tag 25% wide and 20 increments high.
〈HR WIDTH="25%" SIZE=20〉

A Horizontal Rule tag 10% wide and 30 increments high.
〈HR WIDTH="10%" SIZE=30〉

A Horizontal Rule tag without attributes and values.
〈HR〉

〈/BODY〉
〈/HTML〉
```

Enter these tags as
shown here.

Figure 2.9
Insert these internal linking tags.

THINKING ABOUT TECHNOLOGY

Can you figure out how to create an internal hypertext link that will
allow you to move from the bottom of your document to the very top?
Use the same steps you learned in this activity to create a link just
before the 〈/BODY〉 tag that will take you to the top of the page. Your
link should look like this: Top of Page. Resave your extra-effort work
as *TenToTop.html*.

  Why do you think a link back to the top of a page would be valuable?

ACTIVITY

2.4

Objective:
In this activity, you will create links to Web sites with information about HTML, JavaScript, and other languages used on the Web.

Creating Hypertext Links to the Web

The thing that first made the WWW popular was the ability to jump from one page to another anywhere in the world. Before you can do this, however, you must know all about URLs. URLs are Uniform Resource Locators. URLs allow a Web browser to pinpoint an exact file on the Web. The concept is really quite simple.

Have you ever seen a URL similar to this sample?

http://www.swep.com/webpagefolder/anotherfolder/afileyouwant.html

When you enter a URL (Uniform Resource Locator) into your HTML Web page, you are identifying a path to a specific HTML file located somewhere in cyberspace. This file may be on your local computer or somewhere on the Web.

You often can see the name of a file at the end of a URL. Look at the end of our sample URL. The file name *afileyouwant.html* is the name of an HTML file (*afileyouwant*). The **.html** extension identifies the file as an HTML document that your Web browser can display.

However, before you can get to *afileyouwant.html*, you need to know the path or the way to this file name. The key in finding the file name's path is in the URL or Web address. Let's see what this means by breaking down the sample URL into its various parts.

In some URLs, you may see the letters *http* followed by a colon and a couple of slashes. The *http://* tells your network how to transfer or move the file you are requesting. The **HTTP** stands for **Hypertext Transfer Protocol**. A **protocol** is a communications system that is used to transfer data over networks. It is like a secret digital language that Web servers use to communicate with Web browsers.

The second part of the address (*www.swep.com*) is the actual name of the server that hosts the Web page for which you are looking. The *www* stands for the World Wide Web. The www tells you that this server uses Web technology. The *.swep* part is the name of the company that maintains the Web server. In this case, *swep* is short for the South-Western Educational Publishing. The *.com* says this is a commercial or business site. You may see other addresses that are marked as *.edu* for education, or *.gov* for government Web sites.

The slashes and names in the rest of the URL (*/webpagefolder/ anotherfolder/*) represent folders on the Web computer. These are also called subdirectories. You have subdirectories on your computer also. Figure 2.10 shows how folders are organized on a Windows computer. All computers use some sort of folder system to organize files. If you want to find a file on a computer, you need to know the path through the many possible folders in which the file is hidden. Knowing the path is the key to finding the Web page you want.

Before you can find a Web site's welcome page, you need to know the URL. In this activity, you will enter URLs for some of the most important companies in the race to create a better, more exciting

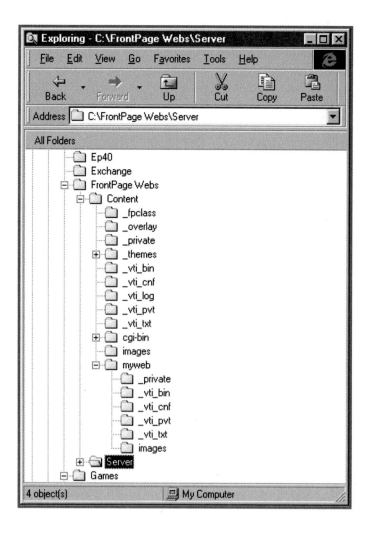

Figure 2.10
A Windows folder or subdirectory organization

Web. Many of these sites have information on HTML, JavaScript, and other important Web tools. They include:

http://www.microsoft.com   *http://www.sun.com*
http://home.netscape.com   *http://www.oracle.com*

1 Open your *Ten.html* file.

2 Create a hypertext link (as shown here and in bold in Figure 2.11) from the list near the top of the page and the new section you are creating.

⟨BR⟩⟨**A HREF="#HYPERLINKS"**⟩Hyperlinks to HTML and JavaScript Sources⟨**/A**⟩

3 Add a new level 2 heading with the words *Hyperlinks to HTML and JavaScript Sources* just below the last ⟨HR⟩ tag of your Web page and just before the ⟨/BODY⟩ tag, as shown in Figure 2.11. Include the ⟨A NAME⟩ tag so you can create an internal hypertext link from the link you created in Step 2.

⟨**P**⟩⟨**H2**⟩⟨**A NAME= "hyperlinks"**⟩ **Hyperlinks to HTML and JavaScript Sources**⟨**/A**⟩⟨**/H2**⟩⟨**/P**⟩

④ Below your new heading and before the ⟨/BODY⟩ tag, create the following hypertext links exactly as shown here and in bold in Figure 2.11.

⟨BR⟩⟨A HREF="http://www.microsoft.com"⟩Microsoft⟨/A⟩
⟨BR⟩⟨A HREF="http://home.netscape.com"⟩Netscape⟨/A⟩
⟨BR⟩⟨A HREF="http://www.sun.com"⟩Sun Microsystems⟨/A⟩
⟨BR⟩⟨A HREF="http://www.oracle.com"⟩Oracle⟨/A⟩

Figure 2.11
Hypertext linking tags

```
⟨HTML⟩
⟨TITLE⟩HTML and JavaScript⟨/TITLE⟩

⟨BODY BGCOLOR=WHITE⟩
⟨CENTER⟩⟨H1⟩Organizing Tags⟨/H1⟩⟨/CENTER⟩

⟨P⟩There are many ways to organize a Web page. This Web page will organize text, hypertext links, colors,
and fonts. It will also demonstrate single spacing, double spacing, and the use of line breaks.⟨/P⟩

⟨P⟩This Web page will display how to organize Web pages in a number of ways using: ⟨/P⟩

⟨BR⟩⟨A HREF="#POWERFUL"⟩Powerful Lines⟨/A⟩
⟨BR⟩⟨A HREF="#HYPERLINKS"⟩Hyperlinks to HTML and JavaScript Sources⟨/A⟩
⟨BR⟩Hyperlinks to Previously Created Web Pages
⟨BR⟩Fancy Fonts
⟨BR⟩Perfect Pictures
⟨BR⟩Orderly Tables                        New Internal Page Link
⟨BR⟩Extraordinary Extras

⟨HR⟩
⟨P⟩⟨H2⟩⟨A NAME="POWERFUL"⟩Powerful Lines⟨/A⟩⟨/H2⟩⟨/P⟩

A Horizontal Rule tag 50% wide and 10 increments high.
⟨HR WIDTH="50%" SIZE=10⟩

A Horizontal Rule tag 25% wide and 20 increments high.
⟨HR WIDTH="25%" SIZE=20⟩

A Horizontal Rule tag 10% wide and 30 increments high.
⟨HR WIDTH="10%" SIZE=30⟩

A Horizontal Rule tag without attributes and values.
⟨HR⟩

⟨P⟩⟨H2⟩⟨A NAME="HYPERLINKS"⟩ Hyperlinks to HTML and JavaScript Sources ⟨/A⟩⟨/H2⟩⟨/P⟩

⟨BR⟩⟨A HREF="http://www.microsoft.com"⟩Microsoft⟨/A⟩
⟨BR⟩⟨A HREF="http://home.netscape.com"⟩Netscape⟨/A⟩               Hypertext Links
⟨BR⟩⟨A HREF="http://www.sun.com"⟩Sun Microsystems⟨/A⟩           to the Web
⟨BR⟩⟨A HREF="http://www.oracle.com"⟩Oracle⟨/A⟩

⟨/BODY⟩
⟨/HTML⟩
```

5 Your entire page of tags should now appear as those in Figure 2.11. Save your work as *Eleven.html*.

6 View your work in your Web browser. Your new links should look like Figure 2.12.

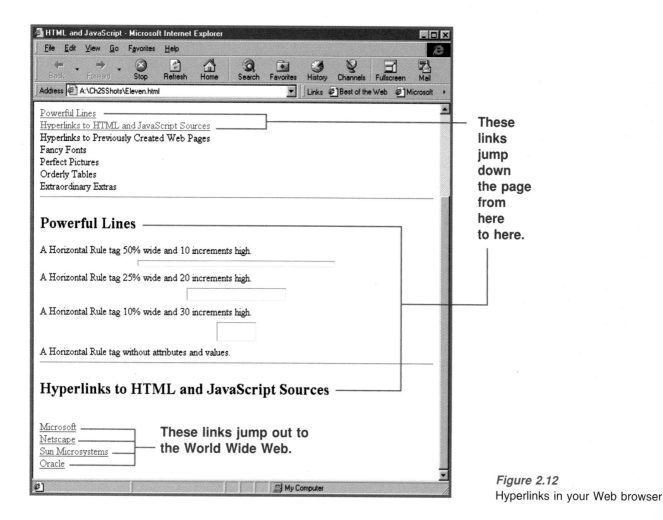

These links jump down the page from here to here.

Figure 2.12
Hyperlinks in your Web browser

7 If you have a live connection to the Web, try your links and see if they work! (Note: If your links don't work properly, carefully review your tags and make any necessary corrections. Resave your work. Then, reload or refresh your page in your Web browser and try again. Remember that your browser won't look for your newly corrected Web page unless you tell it to. You can do this in a couple of ways. You can open the page again, or you can click on the *Reload* or *Refresh* buttons to load an updated copy of your Web page into your browser.)

THINKING ABOUT TECHNOLOGY

What are the ten most important Web sites? What makes them important to you? Create a new HTML page that indexes and lists your most important personal Web pages. Call the page *My Web Resources*. Keep adding to your Web resources page as you work through this text.

ACTIVITY

2.5

Objective:
In this activity, you will create links to Web pages you have previously created.

Linking to Pages You've Already Created

In this activity, you will link to the first eleven HTML pages you have already created in this course. Keeping track of all of your pages in this way will help you quickly review the progress you have made.

1 Open your *Eleven.html* file.

2 Create a hypertext link from your list near the top of the page and the new section you are creating. The text to be entered is shown in bold here and in Figure 2.13.

⟨BR⟩**⟨A HREF="#PREVIOUS"⟩**Hyperlinks to Previously Created Web Pages⟨/**A**⟩

3 Create a new ⟨**HR**⟩ tag, as shown in Figure 2.13, following your list of Web links you created in Activity 2.3.

4 As shown in Figure 2.13, add a new level 2 heading called *Hyperlinks to Previously Created Web Pages* just below the new HR tag you just created, and just before the ⟨/BODY⟩ tag. Include the ⟨A NAME⟩ tag so you can link to this exact spot from the tag you created in Step 3.

⟨**HR**⟩
⟨**P**⟩⟨**H2**⟩⟨**A NAME= "PREVIOUS"⟩Hyperlinks to Previously Created Web Pages**⟨/**A**⟩⟨/**H2**⟩⟨/**P**⟩

5 Below the new heading near the end of your document, create the hypertext links exactly as shown here and in bold in Figure 2.13.

⟨**BR**⟩⟨**A HREF="One.html"⟩One**⟨/**A**⟩
⟨**BR**⟩⟨**A HREF="Two.html"⟩Two**⟨/**A**⟩
⟨**BR**⟩⟨**A HREF="Three.html"⟩Three**⟨/**A**⟩
⟨**BR**⟩⟨**A HREF="Four.html"⟩Four**⟨/**A**⟩
⟨**BR**⟩⟨**A HREF="Five.html"⟩Five**⟨/**A**⟩
⟨**BR**⟩⟨**A HREF="Six.html"⟩Six**⟨/**A**⟩
⟨**BR**⟩⟨**A HREF="Seven.html"⟩Seven**⟨/**A**⟩
⟨**BR**⟩⟨**A HREF="Eight.html"⟩Eight**⟨/**A**⟩
⟨**BR**⟩⟨**A HREF="Nine.html"⟩Nine**⟨/**A**⟩
⟨**BR**⟩⟨**A HREF="Ten.html"⟩Ten**⟨/**A**⟩
⟨**BR**⟩⟨**A HREF="Eleven.html"⟩Eleven**⟨/**A**⟩

6 Your entire page of tags should now appear like those in Figure 2.13. Save your work as *Twelve.html*.

NET TIP

Capital Mistakes

YOU HAVE PROBABLY BEEN TOLD THAT CAPITAL LETTERS IN AN EMAIL OR NEWSGROUP MESSAGE IS CONSIDERED SHOUTING. ON A WEB PAGE, ENTERING TEXT IN CAPITAL LETTERS IS NOT CONSIDERED SHOUTING. INSTEAD, CAPITAL LETTERS ALLOW YOU TO EMPHASIZE TEXT.

HOWEVER, CAPITAL LETTERS OFTEN MAKE TEXT HARD TO READ. THE USE OF CAPITAL LETTERS SHOULD BE RESERVED FOR HEADINGS OR FOR IMPORTANT WORDS YOU WANT READERS TO NOTICE. PARAGRAPHS THAT APPEAR IN ALL CAPITAL LETTERS ARE HARD TO READ! SO, USE CAPITAL LETTERS SPARINGLY.

```
〈HTML〉
〈TITLE〉HTML and JavaScript〈/TITLE〉

〈BODY BGCOLOR=WHITE〉
〈CENTER〉〈H1〉Organizing Tags〈/H1〉〈/CENTER〉

〈P〉There are many ways to organize a Web page. This Web page will organize text, hypertext links, colors, and fonts.
It will also demonstrate single spacing, double spacing, and the use of line breaks.〈/P〉

〈P〉This Web page will display how to organize Web pages in a number of ways using: 〈/P〉

〈BR〉〈A HREF="#POWERFUL")Powerful Lines〈/A〉
〈BR〉〈A HREF="#HYPERLINKS")Hyperlinks to HTML and JavaScript Sources〈/A〉
〈BR〉 〈A HREF="#PREVIOUS"〉Hyperlinks to Previously Created Web Pages〈/A〉
〈BR〉Fancy Fonts
〈BR〉Perfect Pictures
〈BR〉Orderly Tables
〈BR〉Extraordinary Extras

〈HR〉
〈P〉〈H2〉〈A NAME= "POWERFUL")Powerful Lines〈/A〉〈/H2〉〈/P〉

A Horizontal Rule tag 50% wide and 10 increments high.
〈HR WIDTH="50%" SIZE=10〉

A Horizontal Rule tag 25% wide and 20 increments high.
〈HR WIDTH="25%" SIZE=20〉

A Horizontal Rule tag 10% wide and 30 increments high.
〈HR WIDTH="10%" SIZE=30〉

A Horizontal Rule tag without attributes and values.
〈HR〉

〈P〉〈H2〉〈A NAME= "HYPERLINKS")Hyperlinks to HTML and JavaScript Sources
〈/A〉〈/H2〉〈/P〉

〈BR〉〈A HREF="http://www.microsoft.com")Microsoft〈/A〉
〈BR〉〈A HREF="http://home.netscape.com")Netscape〈/A〉
〈BR〉〈A HREF="http://www.sun.com")Sun Microsystems〈/A〉
〈BR〉〈A HREF="http://www.oracle.com")Oracle〈/A〉

〈HR〉
〈P〉〈H2〉〈A NAME= "PREVIOUS"〉 Hyperlinks to Previously Created Web Pages〈/A〉〈/H2〉〈/P〉

〈BR〉〈A HREF="One.html")One〈/A〉
〈BR〉〈A HREF="Two.html")Two〈/A〉
〈BR〉〈A HREF="Three.html")Three〈/A〉
〈BR〉〈A HREF="Four.html")Four〈/A〉
〈BR〉〈A HREF="Five.html")Five〈/A〉
〈BR〉〈A HREF="Six.html")Six〈/A〉
〈BR〉〈A HREF="Seven.html")Seven〈/A〉
〈BR〉〈A HREF="Eight.html")Eight〈/A〉
〈BR〉〈A HREF="Nine.html")Nine〈/A〉
〈BR〉〈A HREF="Ten.html")Ten〈/A〉
〈BR〉〈A HREF="Eleven.html")Eleven〈/A〉

〈/BODY〉
〈/HTML〉
```

Figure 2.13
Creating links to Web pages
you have created

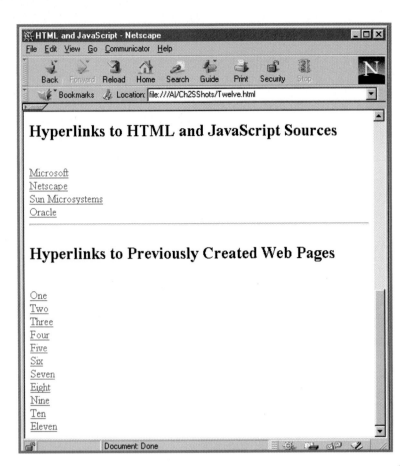

Hyperlinks to HTML and JavaScript Sources

Microsoft
Netscape
Sun Microsystems
Oracle

Hyperlinks to Previously Created Web Pages

One
Two
Three
Four
Five
Six
Seven
Eight
Nine
Ten
Eleven

Figure 2.14
Links to previously created
Web pages

7 View your work in your Web browser. Your new links should look like Figure 2.14. Test each link and make sure they all work. Make any corrections that are necessary. (Note: Once again, if your links don't work properly, review your tags, make any necessary corrections, and resave your work. Then, reload or refresh the page in your Web browser.)

THINKING ABOUT TECHNOLOGY

Now that you have created lists of hypertext links, how can you turn your lists into bulleted and numbered lists? Try using the ⟨OL⟩, ⟨UL⟩, and ⟨LI⟩ tags to turn your hyperlinks into bulleted and numbered lists.

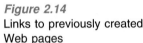

Internet Milestone

HTML Standards

HTML is a powerful tool because it allows all kinds of computers to display Web pages. With HTML, it doesn't matter if you are running a Macintosh or a Windows machine. You can even be on a UNIX workstation or some other type of computer.

The reason HTML Web pages are able to be seen by all types of computers is that HTML guardians maintain a certain set of standards that all Web browser makers voluntarily follow. New standards and new HTML tags and commands are being added all the time. Each new tag is submitted to a standards committee who reviews it. Every now and then, enough new commands are added to HTML that a new version of HTML appears. These versions are marked by numbers, HTML 1, HTML 2, HTML 3, HTML 4, and so on.

You can learn more about HTML standards and receive help expanding your HTML skills online. Go to your search engine and try these search words.

HTML Standards
HTML Standards Committee
HTML 1
HTML 2
HTML 3
HTML 4
HTML 5
HTML Learning
HTML Guides

ACTIVITY
2.6

Objective:
In this activity, you will change the color attributes for text, links, and visited links.

As you have surfed the Web, you may have noticed that the text colors often change from page to page. In Activity 2.1, you changed the background color of your Web page by inserting the YELLOW value into the BGCOLOR=attribute in the ⟨BODY⟩ tag. Then you changed the background to several other colors. Changing text color is just as easy.

There are three basic types of text color you can change:

Type of Text	Attribute
• The text itself	TEXT=
• The hypertext link color	LINK=
• The visited link color (or the links you have already selected)	VLINK=

1. Open your *Twelve.html* file.

2. In the body tag at the beginning of the Web page, leave the BGCOLOR as WHITE, but make the TEXT=BLUE, the LINK=RED, and the VLINK=GREEN, as shown in Figure 2.15.

```
⟨HTML⟩
⟨TITLE⟩HTML and JavaScript⟨/TITLE⟩

⟨BODY   BGCOLOR=WHITE   TEXT=BLUE   LINK=RED   VLINK=GREEN⟩
```

Figure 2.15
Creating links to your previous Web pages

3. Save your work as *Thirteen.html*.

NET TIP

Looking for HTML Errors

Proofreading HTML tags can be difficult. Even the slightest error can drastically change the look and organization of a Web page. Here are some common things to look for.

- *Make sure all your angle brackets ⟨ and ⟩ are facing in the proper direction.*
- *Often, Web page writers mis-use the shift key when making angle brackets or creating a slash.*
This results in a comma, a period, or a question mark where the slash or angle bracket should appear.
- *If all the text appears centered, perhaps you forgot the close ⟨/CENTER⟩ tag.*
- *If you want a double space instead of a single space, use a ⟨P⟩ tag instead of a ⟨BR⟩ tag.*
- *If bullets appear long after a list, perhaps you forgot*
the close unordered list tag, ⟨/UL⟩.
- *Many times quotation marks are required to identify values. If a value doesn't work, check to see if "quotation" marks are needed.*
- *Make sure you save your file each time you make a correction to a Web page.*
- *Don't forget that Web pages must be reloaded or refreshed before changes can take effect.*

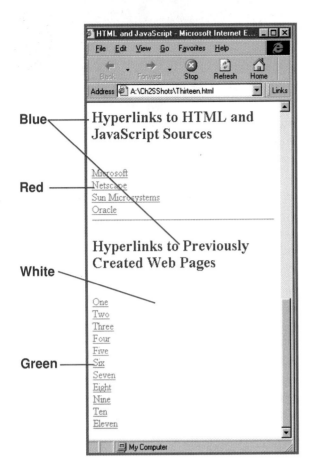

Blue

Red

White

Green

Figure 2.16
Changing text colors

④ View your work in your Web browser. Your page should appear with blue text, red hyperlinks, and green visited links on a white background as seen in Figure 2.16.

THINKING ABOUT TECHNOLOGY

Try experimenting by substituting hexadecimal number values listed below for the names of colors in the 〈BODY〉 tag. Use the number or pound (#) sign before your number. See *Net Fact: Hexadecimal Colors.* Some of the most common hexadecimal number values are:

RED   = #FF0000
GREEN   = #00FF00
BLUE   = #0000FF
WHITE   = #FFFFFF
BLACK   = #000000
YELLOW = #FFFF00

Net Fun

Another fun tag is the marquee tag. Anything you put between the marquee tags, 〈MARQUEE〉〈/MARQUEE〉, will scroll across the screen like a stock market ticker. The tag was designed for the Internet Explorer browser by Microsoft, and doesn't work on every browser. Experiment, and see what happens. In the right browser, it's cool!

NET VOCABULARY

Define the following terms:

1. attributes

2. fonts

3. hexadecimal

4. HTTP

5. hyperlinks

6. hypertext links

7. Hypertext Transfer Protocol

8. values

NET REVIEW

Give a short answer to the following questions:

1. What tag will make words FLASH on and off repeatedly?

2. What hexadecimal value will create the color yellow?

3. Which tags do you know of that do not need a closing tag in order to work effectively?

4. What are three common HTML errors?

5. *What do the letters in RESPECT stand for?*

_____

_____

_____

6. *Why are there different versions of HTML?*

_____

_____

_____

_____

_____

_____

THE SEVEN MOST UNORGANIZED PAGES
ON THE NET

In Chapter 1's Net Project Teamwork exercise, you identified seven of the greatest Web pages you could find. In this Net Project, Great Applications, Inc. wants you to identify the seven worst pages you can find. These pages are to be used in a training seminar to help new employees learn how to create high-quality Web pages. Your manager suggested that you surf the Web and find seven examples of hard-to-read, unorganized, or boring Web pages to show new interns exactly what *not* to do.

Surf the Web looking for awful Web page examples. Record the title and URL of each page and write a brief summary explaining in your own words why these pages are horrible!

Title that Appears in the Title bar	Web Address or URL	Summary of the Reasons Why These Pages Are Poor Quality

---

NET PROJECT TEAMWORK   **Building a Product Information Page**

Great Applications, Inc. is holding a design contest to see who can build the most informative and organized Web pages. Specifically, they are looking for a team that can create Web pages that introduce new products to customers over the Web.

The contest gives teams of three to five people two hours to create an informative Web page about a product of their choice. Form your team, and brainstorm a new product to introduce. It could be a new CD or a new computer game. It could be a new fashion or a new car. For the purpose of this contest, it doesn't really matter the product you pick, so don't take up too much of your time deciding what product you will use.

Create your team's Web page contest entry. Divide up the writing responsibilities. Have one person enter the basic tags and serve as Webmaster. Have each team member research and write a portion of the Web page. Collaborate by editing and revising each other's writing and HTML tags. Use the techniques you have learned in this chapter to organize the information you wish to present.

We all know that teamwork is important. However, are there times when teamwork is harder than working alone? Answer the following questions about teams creating Web pages together.

As you worked together in a team in the Net Project Teamwork activity, what problems did you encounter?

_____

_____

_____

_____

_____

How did you organize your team? How did you divide up the work? Which team members were responsible for which activities?

_____

_____

_____

_____

_____

_____

Did teamwork create a better Web page? If so, how?

_____

_____

_____

_____

_____

What advice would you give to other teams who are trying to create Web pages together?

_____

_____

_____

_____

_____

_____

HTML Power Techniques

Chapter Objectives

In this chapter, you will add styles and special effects to your Web page. After reading Chapter 3, you will be able to

1. control the size, style, and color of fonts.

2. download pictures from the Web.

3. insert pictures into your Web page.

4. change the size of graphics.

5. use tables to organize information.

6. turn pictures into hyperlinks.

7. insert a variety of data input options into a Web page.

HTML Terms

.gif

.jpg or .jpeg

fonts

graphics

Graphics Interchange Format

image

Joint Photographic Expert Group

table cell

The Exciting Web

The Web is full of pictures, sounds, and movies that add interest to Web pages. Generally, there are two kinds of pictures (called **graphics** or **images**) on the WWW. They include **.gif** files (**Graphics Interchange Format**) and **.jpg** or **.jpeg** (**Joint Photographic Expert Group**) files. The extensions .gif and .jpg help tell your browser that these files are pictures, not .html text files, and require special handling.

The more you learn about HTML, the more you can add exciting new effects and styles to your Web page. As we mentioned in Chapter 2, **fonts**, or the style of letters, can be changed. Every font has a style all its own.

By using the ⟨FONT⟩ tag's many attributes and values, you can manipulate fonts in millions of ways.

Tables allow the parts of a Web page to be divided up, creating special spaces for each new element or piece of information you may want to include.

Tables, fonts, and pictures can add power to your pages. In this chapter, you will learn to manipulate these special HTML features. You will also learn about some extraordinary input tags that will allow visitors to your Web page to interact with your Web page. ■

ACTIVITY

3.1

Objective:

In this activity, you will change font style, size, and color.

Font Attributes and Values

When you change text colors in the ⟨BODY⟩ tag, as you did in Activity 2.6, you change the color of your words for the entire page. If you want to have more control (that is, if you want to change the size, color, or style of a single paragraph, a single sentence, or even a single word), use the ⟨FONT⟩ tag.

Use the ⟨FONT⟩ tag's attributes to control:

- The size of words with the SIZE attribute ⟨FONT SIZE=#⟩
- The style of words with the FACE attribute ⟨FONT FACE=#⟩
- The color of words with the COLOR attribute ⟨FONT COLOR=#⟩

1 Open your *Thirteen.html* file.

2 Create a hypertext link in the list near the top of the page that will hyperlink to the new section you will be creating in this activity. The text to be entered is shown in bold here and in Figure 3.1.

⟨BR⟩**⟨A HREF="#FONTS"⟩**Fancy Fonts⟨**/A**⟩

3 Create a new ⟨**HR**⟩ tag, as shown in Figure 3.1, following the list of Web page links you created in Activity 2.5.

4 As shown in Figure 3.1, add a new level 2 heading called *Fancy Fonts* just below the new ⟨HR⟩ tag you just created, and just before the ⟨/BODY⟩ tag. Include the ⟨A NAME⟩ tag to finish the internal hypertext link you started in Step 2.

⟨HR⟩
⟨P⟩⟨H2⟩⟨A NAME="FONTS"⟩ Fancy Fonts ⟨/A⟩⟨/H2⟩⟨/P⟩

5 Below the new heading, near the end of your document, enter the font tags, attributes, and values exactly as shown here and in bold in Figure 3.1.

⟨BR⟩**⟨FONT FACE=HELVETICA SIZE=4 COLOR=RED⟩This is the Helvetica font at Size 4**⟨/FONT⟩
⟨BR⟩**⟨FONT FACE=TIMES SIZE=6 COLOR=GREEN⟩This is the Times font at Size 6**⟨/FONT⟩
⟨BR⟩**⟨FONT FACE=ARIAL SIZE=8 COLOR=ORANGE⟩This is the Arial font at Size 8**⟨/FONT⟩
⟨BR⟩**⟨FONT FACE=COURIER SIZE=2 COLOR=BLACK⟩This is the Courier font at Size 2**⟨/FONT⟩

6 Your tags should now appear like those in Figure 3.1. Save your work as *Fourteen.html*.

NET TIP

Adding Emphasis

There are other ways to change the look of text. Try these tags around certain words and see what effect they create. Can you guess what they do?

⟨B⟩⟨/B⟩
⟨EM⟩⟨/EM⟩
⟨STRONG⟩⟨/STRONG⟩
⟨I⟩⟨/I⟩

```
⟨HTML⟩
⟨TITLE⟩HTML and JavaScript⟨/TITLE⟩

⟨BODY BGCOLOR=WHITE TEXT=BLUE LINK=RED VLINK=GREEN⟩
⟨CENTER⟩⟨H1⟩Organizing Tags⟨/H1⟩ ⟨/CENTER⟩

⟨P⟩There are many ways to organize a Web page. This Web page will organize text, hypertext links, colors, and fonts. It will also demonstrate single spacing, double spacing, and the use of line breaks.⟨/P⟩

⟨P⟩This Web page will display how to organize Web pages in a number of ways using: ⟨/P⟩

⟨BR⟩⟨A HREF="#POWERFUL"⟩Powerful Lines⟨/A⟩
⟨BR⟩⟨A HREF="#HYPERLINKS"⟩Hyperlinks to HTML and JavaScript sources⟨/A⟩
⟨BR⟩⟨A HREF="#PREVIOUS"⟩Hyperlinks to previously created Web pages⟨/A⟩
⟨BR⟩⟨A HREF="#FONTS"⟩Fancy Fonts⟨/A⟩
⟨BR⟩Perfect Pictures
⟨BR⟩Orderly Tables
⟨BR⟩Extraordinary Extras

⟨HR⟩
⟨P⟩⟨H2⟩⟨A NAME= "POWERFUL"⟩Powerful Lines⟨/A⟩⟨/H2⟩⟨/P⟩

A Horizontal Rule tag 50% wide and 10 increments high.
⟨HR WIDTH="50%" SIZE=10⟩

A Horizontal Rule tag 25% wide and 20 increments high.
⟨HR WIDTH="25%" SIZE=20⟩

A Horizontal Rule tag 10% wide and 30 increments high.
⟨HR WIDTH="10%" SIZE=30⟩

A Horizontal Rule tag without attributes and values.
⟨HR⟩

⟨P⟩⟨H2⟩⟨A NAME="HYPERLINKS"⟩Hyperlinks to HTML and JavaScript sources⟨/A⟩⟨/H2⟩⟨/P⟩

⟨BR⟩⟨A HREF="http://www.microsoft.com"⟩Microsoft⟨/A⟩
⟨BR⟩⟨A HREF="http://home.netscape.com"⟩Netscape⟨/A⟩
⟨BR⟩⟨A HREF="http://www.sun.com"⟩Sun Microsystems⟨/A⟩
⟨BR⟩⟨A HREF="http://www.oracle.com"⟩Oracle⟨/A⟩

⟨HR⟩
⟨P⟩⟨H2⟩⟨A NAME= "PREVIOUS"⟩ Hyperlinks to previously created Web pages⟨/A⟩⟨/H2⟩⟨/P⟩

⟨BR⟩⟨A HREF="One.html"⟩One⟨/A⟩
⟨BR⟩⟨A HREF="Two.html"⟩Two⟨/A⟩
⟨BR⟩⟨A HREF="Three.html"⟩Three⟨/A⟩
⟨BR⟩⟨A HREF="Four.html"⟩Four⟨/A⟩
⟨BR⟩⟨A HREF="Five.html"⟩Five⟨/A⟩
⟨BR⟩⟨A HREF="Six.html"⟩Six⟨/A⟩
⟨BR⟩⟨A HREF="Seven.html"⟩Seven⟨/A⟩
⟨BR⟩⟨A HREF="Eight.html"⟩Eight⟨/A⟩
⟨BR⟩⟨A HREF="Nine.html"⟩Nine⟨/A⟩
⟨BR⟩⟨A HREF="Ten.html"⟩Ten⟨/A⟩
⟨BR⟩⟨A HREF="Eleven.html"⟩Eleven⟨/A⟩

⟨HR⟩
⟨P⟩⟨H2⟩⟨A NAME= "FONTS"⟩ Fancy Fonts ⟨/A⟩⟨/H2⟩⟨/P⟩

⟨BR⟩⟨FONT FACE=HELVETICA SIZE=4 COLOR=RED⟩This is the Helvetica font at Size 4⟨/FONT⟩
⟨BR⟩⟨FONT FACE=TIMES SIZE=6 COLOR=GREEN⟩This is the Times font at Size 6⟨/FONT⟩
⟨BR⟩⟨FONT FACE=ARIAL SIZE=8 COLOR=ORANGE⟩This is the Arial font at Size 8⟨/FONT⟩
⟨BR⟩⟨FONT FACE=COURIER SIZE=2 COLOR=BLACK⟩This is the Courier font at Size 2⟨/FONT⟩

⟨/BODY⟩
⟨/HTML⟩
```

Figure 3.1
Applying font styles, sizes, and colors

7 View your work in your Web browser. Your changes should look like Figure 3.2. Make any corrections that appear necessary.

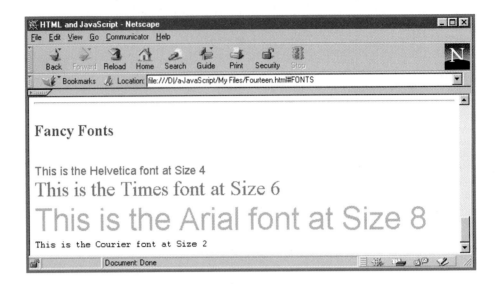

Figure 3.2
Various font styles, sizes, and colors

THINKING ABOUT TECHNOLOGY

You can make your pages nicer by changing font size, font colors, and font faces. What other font changes can you make? Try changing the font styles, colors, and sizes in the introductory paragraphs in your *Fourteen.html* Web page. Try several new font colors and font face combinations. Try various font sizes from 1 to 9. Save your new work as *Fourteen-2.html.*

It is easy to create a way for your readers to respond to your Web page in an e-mail message. Simply use the *mailto* tag that looks like this, ⟨A HREF="mailto:your_email@address"⟩ Your Name⟨/A⟩. When your users click the link, an e-mail form will appear. Not every Web browser is set up properly to handle this *mailto* tag, so experiment. You may need some help from your local Webmaster before you can actually send mail.

Downloading and Inserting Graphics

ACTIVITY
3.2

Objective:
In this activity, you will download a graphic from the Web and insert it into a Web page.

Pictures can be found in many places. You can find pictures in your clip art collection, scan pictures into your computer with a scanner, draw your own pictures, or copy them from the Web. However, before you can easily use pictures in your Web pages, you need to convert them into one of the acceptable Web formats. These commonly include:

- .gif
- .jpg or .jpeg

The first type of graphics or image format, **.gif**, was originally created by CompuServe to provide a compressed graphics format that could transfer easily over low-speed modems. The **Graphics Interchange Format** is usually abbreviated as GIF. There is some debate on how to say GIF. In some parts of the country it is pronounced GIF as in Kathy Lee GIFford. In other parts of the country it is pronounced GIF as in JIFfy Peanut Butter. Either pronunciation works. After all, the pronunciation doesn't change the file format in the least.

The second commonly used format is **.jpg** or **.jpeg**. It is pronounced J-Peg by Webmasters in the know. JPEG is short for **Joint Photographic Expert Group**. This format adheres to an international set of graphics standards. JPEG graphics, like GIF pictures, are compact enough for Internet use.

There are other graphic file formats emerging on the Web. But if you know how to work with these two formats, you will know how to work with any other picture format on the WWW.

Artists on the Web

Artists are in great demand among Web site development companies. There was a time when a Web page would be entirely made up of words or text. Today, pictures seem to dominate Web pages, attracting a greater number of visitors than ever before.

If you are considering an artistic career, consider the Web. You may find that most of your artwork will end up on the Web. Big corporations with Web sites and Web site developers are always on the lookout for great artists.

You can create your art using any medium or method you like. Scanners can take your pictures and convert them into digital images. Digital files can be converted into formats that will work on the Web. You can also use a variety of art software to create your works of art or to improve any art you have scanned into Web images.

The best training for a Web artist would be to take as many art classes as you can. The graphics tools you need to use to convert your artwork are easily learned. The skills of an artist will take much more time.

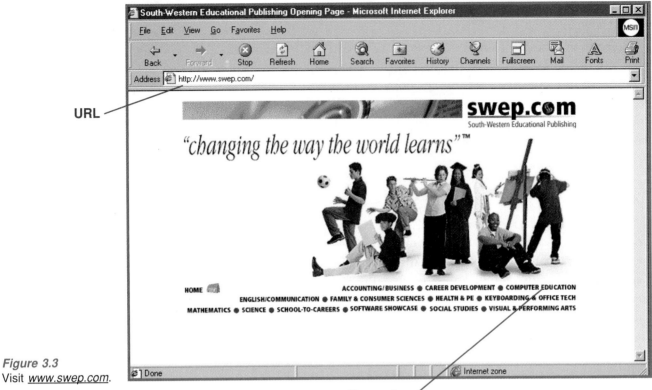

URL

Computer
Education

Figure 3.3
Visit *www.swep.com*.

NET TIP
Shortcut Address

A shortcut URL has been provided to the HTML & JavaScript: Programming Concepts *student activities home page:* htmljava.swep.com.

Figure 3.4
Click on the dragon's nose with the right mouse clicker in Windows, or hold your mouse clicker down on a Macintosh.

1 Open your Web browser.

2 Enter the URL *www.swep.com* in your Web browser.

3 Click on *Computer Education,* as shown in Figure 3.3.

4 Select *Products & Resources* on the left side of the next screen.

5 Select *Internet* from the Computer Education Categories box, and click *Go!*

6 Scroll down and look for the *HTML and JavaScript: Programming Concepts* Web page.

7 Click the Student Activities link.

8 Click on the Activity 3.2: Perfect Pictures link from the list you see. Scroll down until you see a dragon.

9 If you are on a Windows computer, click the right mouse key on the dragon's nose, as shown in Figure 3.4. If you are using a Macintosh, click and hold your mouse key on the dragon's nose.

10 Select the *Save Image As* or *Save Picture As* command from the list that appears, as shown in Figures 3.5a and 3.5b. (Note: The command on your browser may be worded differently. Keep trying the various commands that appear until you find the correct command.)

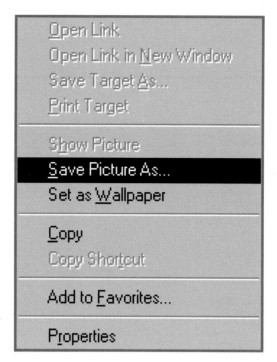

Figure 3.5a
With Netscape, select *Save Image As*

Figure 3.5b
With Internet Explorer, select *Save Picture As*

11 Save your file (called *Levy.gif*) in the *exact same folder* where you have been saving your Web pages.

12 Open your *Fourteen.html* Web page in your word processor or text editor.

13 Create a hypertext link in the list near the top of the page that will hyperlink to the new section you will be creating. The text to be entered is shown in bold here and in Figure 3.6.

⟨BR⟩**⟨A HREF="#PICTURES"⟩**Perfect Pictures⟨**/A⟩**

14 Enter an **⟨HR⟩** tag, as shown in bold in Figure 3.6, after the Fancy Fonts section you created in the previous activity.

15 As shown in Figure 3.6, add a new level 2 heading called *Perfect Pictures* just below the ⟨HR⟩ tag you just created and just before the ⟨/BODY⟩ tag. Include the ⟨A NAME⟩ tag so you can finish the internal hypertext link you started in Step 13.

⟨HR⟩
⟨P⟩⟨H2⟩⟨A NAME= "PICTURES"⟩ Perfect Pictures ⟨/A⟩⟨/H2⟩⟨/P⟩

16 Below your new heading, near the end of your document, enter an Image Source ⟨IMG SRC⟩ tag, as shown here and in Figure 3.6. Notice that the name of the file you just downloaded appears between quotation marks.

⟨IMG SRC="levy.gif"⟩

> **NET TIP**
>
> **A Common Error in the ⟨IMG SRC⟩ Tag**
>
> *IMG SRC is short for IMaGe SouRCe. Many people misuse this tag by transposing the R and the C, and they enter IMG SCR. If you forget the tag, just spell out the words "ImaGe" and "SouRCe" to get the letters in the correct order.*

Your tags should now appear like those in Figure 3.6. If everything looks correct, save your work as *Fifteen.html.*

```
⟨HTML⟩
⟨TITLE⟩HTML and JavaScript⟨/TITLE⟩

⟨BODY BGCOLOR=WHITE TEXT=BLUE
LINK=RED VLINK=GREEN⟩
⟨CENTER⟩⟨H1⟩Organizing Tags⟨/H1⟩⟨/CENTER⟩

⟨P⟩There are many ways to organize a Web page.
This Web page will organize text, hypertext links,
colors, and fonts. It will also demonstrate single
spacing, double spacing, and the use of line
breaks.⟨/P⟩

⟨P⟩This Web page will display how to organize Web
pages in a number of ways using: ⟨/P⟩

⟨BR⟩⟨A HREF="#POWERFUL"⟩Powerful Lines⟨/A⟩
⟨BR⟩⟨A HREF="#HYPERLINKS"⟩Hyperlinks to
HTML and JavaScript sources⟨/A⟩
⟨BR⟩⟨A HREF="#PREVIOUS"⟩Hyperlinks to
previously created Web pages⟨/A⟩
⟨BR⟩⟨A HREF="#FONTS"⟩Fancy Fonts⟨/A⟩
⟨BR⟩⟨A HREF="#PICTURES"⟩Perfect Pictures⟨/A⟩
⟨BR⟩Orderly Tables
⟨BR⟩Extraordinary Extras

⟨HR⟩
⟨P⟩⟨H2⟩⟨A NAME= "POWERFUL"⟩Powerful
Lines⟨/A⟩⟨/H2⟩⟨/P⟩

A Horizontal Rule tag 50% wide and 10 increments
high.
⟨HR WIDTH="50%" SIZE=10⟩

A Horizontal Rule tag 25% wide and 20 increments
high.
⟨HR WIDTH="25%" SIZE=20⟩

A Horizontal Rule tag 10% wide and 30 increments
high.
⟨HR WIDTH="10%" SIZE=30⟩

A Horizontal Rule tag without attributes and values.
⟨HR⟩

⟨P⟩⟨H2⟩⟨A NAME= "HYPERLINKS"⟩Hyperlinks to
HTML and JavaScript sources⟨/A⟩⟨/H2⟩⟨/P⟩
```

```
⟨BR⟩⟨A HREF="http://www.microsoft.com"⟩
Microsoft⟨/A⟩
⟨BR⟩⟨A HREF="http://home.netscape.com"⟩
Netscape⟨/A⟩
⟨BR⟩⟨A HREF="http://www.sun.com"⟩
Sun Microsystems⟨/A⟩
⟨BR⟩⟨A HREF="http://www.oracle.com"⟩
Oracle⟨/A⟩

⟨HR⟩
⟨P⟩⟨H2⟩⟨A NAME= "PREVIOUS"⟩Hyperlinks to
previously created Web pages⟨/A⟩⟨/H2⟩⟨/P⟩

⟨BR⟩⟨A HREF="One.html"⟩One⟨/A⟩
⟨BR⟩⟨A HREF="Two.html"⟩Two⟨/A⟩
⟨BR⟩⟨A HREF="Three.html"⟩Three⟨/A⟩
⟨BR⟩⟨A HREF="Four.html"⟩Four⟨/A⟩
⟨BR⟩⟨A HREF="Five.html"⟩Five⟨/A⟩
⟨BR⟩⟨A HREF="Six.html"⟩Six⟨/A⟩
⟨BR⟩⟨A HREF="Seven.html"⟩Seven⟨/A⟩
⟨BR⟩⟨A HREF="Eight.html"⟩Eight⟨/A⟩
⟨BR⟩⟨A HREF="Nine.html"⟩Nine⟨/A⟩
⟨BR⟩⟨A HREF="Ten.html"⟩Ten⟨/A⟩
⟨BR⟩⟨A HREF="Eleven.html"⟩Eleven⟨/A⟩

⟨HR⟩
⟨P⟩⟨H2⟩⟨A NAME= "FONTS"⟩ Fancy Fonts
⟨/A⟩⟨/H2⟩⟨/P⟩

⟨BR⟩⟨FONT FACE=HELVETICA SIZE=4
COLOR=RED⟩This is the Helvetica font at Size
4⟨/FONT⟩
⟨BR⟩⟨FONT FACE=TIMES SIZE=6 COLOR=
GREEN⟩This is the Times font at Size 6⟨/FONT⟩
⟨BR⟩⟨FONT FACE=ARIAL SIZE=8 COLOR=
ORANGE⟩This is the Arial font at Size 8⟨/FONT⟩
⟨BR⟩⟨FONT FACE=COURIER SIZE=2 COLOR=
BLACK⟩This is the Courier font at Size 2⟨/FONT⟩

⟨HR⟩
⟨P⟩⟨H2⟩⟨A NAME="PICTURES"⟩Perfect Pictures
⟨/A⟩⟨/H2⟩⟨/P⟩

⟨IMG SRC="levy.gif"⟩

⟨/BODY⟩
⟨/HTML⟩
```

Figure 3.6
Inserting a Graphic or Image file

18 View your work in your Web browser. Your picture should look like Figure 3.7, but it may appear larger or smaller in your browser.

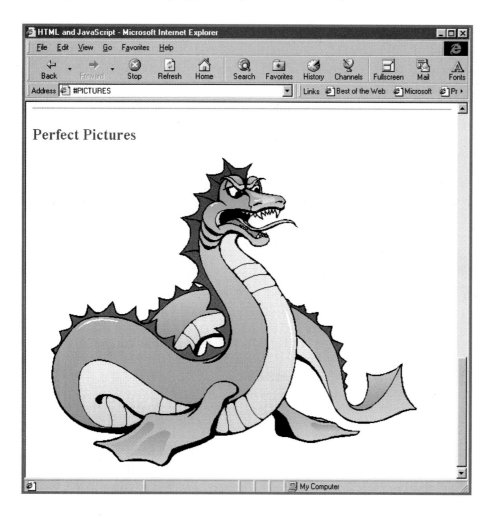

Figure 3.7
Your GIF image as seen in a browser

THINKING ABOUT TECHNOLOGY

How do pictures add or detract from a Web site? Would you ever want to revisit a Web page that doesn't have pictures? Why or why not?

Download another picture and place it in your Web page. Follow steps 1 to 9, but this time, download the picture of Dayna, the dragon fighter found just below Levy the Dragon. Insert this picture into your Web page. Save your new work as *Fifteen-2.html.*

Net Fun

If you are interested in learning more about HTML, you can order HTML books right over the Web. A great place to visit is amazon.com. Amazon.com is the largest bookstore on the World Wide Web. If you can't find the book you are looking for at amazon.com, it probably doesn't exist. Read more about Amazon.com in the Internet Milestone report, *Business on the Web,* p. 65.

ACTIVITY

3.3

Objective:
In this activity, you will manipulate graphic attributes and values.

Pictures of All Sizes

Pictures can be altered in a variety of ways by changing a tag's values. Pictures can be used as wallpaper that cover the entire background of a Web page. They can be aligned in the center, to the left side, or to the right side of a page. They can be made bigger or smaller, depending on your needs.

You can also change the size of the picture by using the HEIGHT and WIDTH attributes. Controlling the exact size of a picture can be very helpful in making a page look sharp and interesting.

In the first part of this activity, you will align your picture to the right of the page and make it small. In the second section, you will line three dragons of varying sizes across the page, and then you will place three dragons vertically down the Web page by manipulating a few tags.

1 Open your *Fifteen.html* file.

2 Near the end of your document, add the following information to your ⟨IMG SRC⟩, tag as shown in bold here and in Figure 3.8.

⟨P⟩⟨IMG SRC="levy.gif" **ALIGN=RIGHT HEIGHT=50 Width=50**⟩⟨/P⟩

3 Save your changes as *Sixteen.html*.

4 View your changes in your Web browser. It should appear as marked in Figure 3.9.

5 Next, create three images that appear across the screen, with each graphic appearing as a different size. To do so, enter the following tags below your first IMG SRC tag, as shown here and in Figure 3.8.

⟨IMG SRC="levy.gif" HEIGHT=100 Width=100⟩
⟨IMG SRC="levy.gif" HEIGHT=150 Width=150⟩
⟨IMG SRC="levy.gif" HEIGHT=200 Width=200⟩

6 Resave your changes (using the same *Sixteen.html* file name) and view your additions in your Web browser. Your changes should appear similar to the three images marked in Figure 3.9. If your graphics don't appear, make any necessary corrections, resave, and view again.

7 Just below the three tags you entered in the previous step, add two more IMG SRC tags, using ⟨P⟩ tags to cause several graphics to appear vertically. Enter these tags exactly as shown here and in Figure 3.8.

⟨P⟩⟨IMG SRC="levy.gif" HEIGHT=150 Width=150⟩⟨/P⟩
⟨P⟩⟨IMG SRC="levy.gif" HEIGHT=200 Width=200⟩⟨/P⟩

8 Resave your changes as *Sixteen.html*, and view the result in your Web browser. Consult Figures 3.8 and 3.9 to evaluate how the tags and graphics should appear. Make corrections where necessary, and review any changes in your browser.

NET TIP

Inserting a Background

To have a picture become your background, insert the BACKGROUND attribute in the ⟨BODY⟩ *tag like this:*

⟨BODY BACKGROUND= "levy.gif"⟩

Try another picture as your background. Make sure the file name appears between the quotation ("   ") marks.

```
⟨HTML⟩
⟨TITLE⟩HTML and JavaScript⟨/TITLE⟩

⟨BODY BGCOLOR=WHITE TEXT=BLUE LINK=
RED VLINK=GREEN⟩
⟨CENTER⟩⟨H1⟩Organizing Tags⟨/H1⟩⟨/CENTER⟩

⟨P⟩There are many ways to organize a Web page.
This Web page will organize text, hypertext links,
colors, and fonts. It will also demonstrate single
spacing, double spacing, and the use of line
breaks.⟨/P⟩

⟨P⟩This Web page will display how to organize Web
pages in a number of ways using: ⟨/P⟩

⟨BR⟩⟨A HREF="#POWERFUL"⟩Powerful Lines⟨/A⟩
⟨BR⟩⟨A HREF="#HYPERLINKS"⟩Hyperlinks to
HTML and JavaScript sources⟨/A⟩
⟨BR⟩⟨A HREF="#PREVIOUS"⟩Hyperlinks to
previously created Web pages⟨/A⟩
⟨BR⟩⟨A HREF="#FONTS"⟩Fancy Fonts⟨/A⟩
⟨BR⟩⟨A HREF="#PICTURES"⟩Perfect Pictures⟨/A⟩
⟨BR⟩Orderly Tables
⟨BR⟩Extraordinary Extras

⟨HR⟩
⟨P⟩⟨H2⟩⟨A NAME="POWERFUL"⟩Powerful Lines⟨/A⟩
⟨/H2⟩⟨/P⟩

A Horizontal Rule tag 50% wide and 10 increments
high.
⟨HR WIDTH="50%"SIZE=10⟩

A Horizontal Rule tag 25% wide and 20 increments
high.
⟨HR WIDTH="25%"SIZE=20⟩

A Horizontal Rule tag 10% wide and 30 increments
high.
⟨HR WIDTH="10%"SIZE=30⟩

A Horizontal Rule tag without
attributes and values.
⟨HR⟩

⟨P⟩⟨H2⟩⟨A NAME= "HYPERLINKS"⟩Hyperlinks to
HTML and JavaScript sources⟨/A⟩⟨/H2⟩⟨/P⟩

⟨BR⟩⟨A HREF="http://www.microsoft.com"⟩
Microsoft⟨/A⟩
⟨BR⟩⟨A HREF="http://home.netscape.com"⟩
Netscape⟨/A⟩
⟨BR⟩⟨A HREF="http://www.sun.com"⟩Sun
Microsystems⟨/A⟩
⟨BR⟩⟨A HREF="http://www.oracle.com"⟩Oracle⟨/A⟩

⟨HR⟩
⟨P⟩⟨H2⟩⟨A NAME= "PREVIOUS"⟩Hyperlinks to
previously created Web pages⟨/A⟩⟨/H2⟩⟨/P⟩

⟨BR⟩⟨A HREF="One.html"⟩One⟨/A⟩
⟨BR⟩⟨A HREF="Two.html"⟩Two⟨/A⟩
⟨BR⟩⟨A HREF="Three.html"⟩Three⟨/A⟩
⟨BR⟩⟨A HREF="Four.html"⟩Four⟨/A⟩
⟨BR⟩⟨A HREF="Five.html"⟩Five⟨/A⟩
⟨BR⟩⟨A HREF="Six.html"⟩Six⟨/A⟩
⟨BR⟩⟨A HREF="Seven.html"⟩Seven⟨/A⟩
⟨BR⟩⟨A HREF="Eight.html"⟩Eight⟨/A⟩
⟨BR⟩⟨A HREF="Nine.html"⟩Nine⟨/A⟩
⟨BR⟩⟨A HREF="Ten.html"⟩Ten⟨/A⟩
⟨BR⟩⟨A HREF="Eleven.html"⟩Eleven⟨/A⟩

⟨HR⟩
⟨P⟩⟨H2⟩⟨A NAME= "FONTS"⟩Fancy Fonts
⟨/A⟩⟨/H2⟩⟨/P⟩

⟨BR⟩⟨FONT FACE=HELVETICA SIZE=4
COLOR=RED⟩This is the Helvetica font at Size 4
⟨/FONT⟩
⟨BR⟩⟨FONT FACE=TIMES SIZE=6
COLOR=GREEN⟩This is the Times font at Size 6
⟨/FONT⟩
⟨BR⟩⟨FONT FACE=ARIAL SIZE=8
COLOR=ORANGE⟩This is the Arial font at Size 8
⟨/FONT⟩
⟨BR⟩⟨FONT FACE=COURIER SIZE=2
COLOR=BLACK⟩This is the Courier font at Size 2
⟨/FONT⟩

⟨HR⟩
⟨P⟩⟨H2⟩⟨A NAME="PICTURES"⟩Perfect Pictures
⟨/A⟩⟨/H2⟩⟨/P⟩

⟨P⟩⟨IMG SRC="levy.gif" ALIGN=RIGHT HEIGHT=50
Width=50⟩⟨/P⟩

⟨IMG SRC="levy.gif" HEIGHT=100 WIDTH=100⟩
⟨IMG SRC="levy.gif" HEIGHT=150 WIDTH=150⟩
⟨IMG SRC="levy.gif" HEIGHT=200 WIDTH=200⟩

⟨P⟩⟨IMG SRC="levy.gif" HEIGHT=150
WIDTH=150⟩⟨/P⟩
⟨P⟩⟨IMG SRC="levy.gif" HEIGHT=200
WIDTH=200⟩⟨/P⟩

⟨/BODY⟩
⟨/HTML⟩
```

Alter this tag in Step 2.

Enter these tags in Step 5.

Enter these tags in Step 7.

Figure 3.8
Dragons everywhere

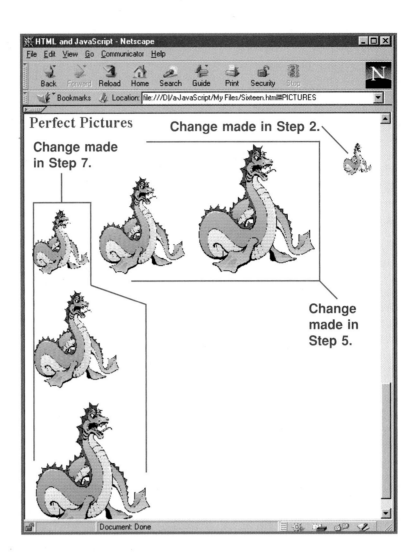

Figure 3.9
Your GIF images after changing the attributes and values

THINKING ABOUT TECHNOLOGY

How fast can you substitute the levy.gif graphic for another graphic? Think about another graphic you like. Find it on the Web and copy it to your Web page folder. (Be sure to check out the *Net Ethics* topic in this activity first!) Change all the *levy.gif* file names in your *Sixteen.html* file to match the name of the new graphic you want to display. For example, replacing levy.gif with dayna.gif will display the dragon slayer in place of the dragon. Manipulate the attributes and values to display your new graphic in a variety of sizes. Save your new work as *Sixteen-2.hmtl.*

Net Ethics   *Picture Piracy*

One of the big problems on the Web is picture piracy. Since it is so easy to pull pictures off the Web, many people do so without permission. Many pictures are copyrighted; that is, someone owns them. To use them, you need to obtain permission or pay a fee to the artist.

Disney has many copyrighted images. They have taken legal action against Web site creators who have illegally used or altered their copyrighted images.

Consider which pictures you download and use from the Web. Are they free for you to use? There are many places that allow the free download of images. For instance, the images you borrowed from the Web site for this book are authorized for your use.

Orderly Tables

Objective:
In this activity, you will create a table and populate its cells with pictures, colors, and various kinds of text.

When you think of a table, well set and ready for a big holiday dinner, you think of how organized everything is. All the place settings, plates, cups, and silverware are well organized and in just the right spot.

Electronic tables are just like that. Tables create little boxes in which you can place things to keep them organized. In this activity, you will create a table and then insert many of the tags you have already learned into its little boxes called **table cells**.

Creating a table is easy with the ⟨TABLE⟩ tag. Cells can have a border by adding a BORDER attribute and a number value. You can also make cells appear larger around pictures and text with the CELLPADDING attribute. Within cells, you can align pictures and text to the center, left, or right.

1. Open your *Sixteen.html* file.

2. Create a hypertext link in your list near the top of the page that will hyperlink to the new section you are creating. The text to be entered is shown in bold here and in Figure 3.10.

   ⟨BR⟩**⟨A HREF="#TABLES"⟩**Orderly Tables**⟨/A⟩**

3. Create a new ⟨**HR**⟩ tag following the graphics you inserted in Activities 3.2 and 3.3.

4. As shown in Figure 3.10, add a new level 2 heading called *Orderly Tables* just below the ⟨HR⟩ tag you just created and just before the ⟨/BODY⟩ tag. Include the ⟨A NAME⟩ tag so you can complete the internal hypertext link you started in Step 2.

   ⟨HR⟩
   ⟨P⟩⟨H2⟩⟨A NAME= "TABLES"⟩ Orderly Tables ⟨/A⟩⟨/H2⟩⟨/P⟩

5. Below the new heading, near the end of your document, enter the ⟨TABLE⟩ tags, attributes, and values, exactly as shown here and in bold in Figure 3.10.

   ⟨TABLE BORDER=5 CELLPADDING=10 ALIGN=CENTER⟩
   ⟨TR⟩
       ⟨TH⟩Dragons⟨/TH⟩
       ⟨TH⟩Colors⟨/TH⟩
       ⟨TH⟩Fonts⟨/TH⟩
   ⟨/TR⟩
   ⟨TR⟩
       ⟨TD⟩⟨IMG SRC="levy.gif" HEIGHT=50 WIDTH=50⟩⟨/TD⟩
       ⟨TD BGCOLOR=RED ALIGN=CENTER⟩Red⟨/TD⟩
       ⟨TD ALIGN=CENTER⟩⟨FONT FACE=TIMES SIZE=7
   COLOR=GREEN⟩Times⟨/TD⟩
   ⟨/TR⟩

NET TIP

Pictures as Hyperlinks

How would you create a hyperlink when the link is a picture? It's easy. Use the same tag structure you used to create hypertext links, but use the IMG SRC tag to replace the words you would normally enter. Try it!

⟨P⟩⟨A HREF="One.html"⟩
⟨IMG SRC="levy.gif"
HEIGHT=50
WIDTH=50⟩⟨/A⟩

This link will open the first page you created with this book. Think about how much you have learned since then!

⟨TR⟩
　　⟨TD⟩⟨IMG SRC="levy.gif" HEIGHT=75 WIDTH=50⟩⟨/TD⟩
　　⟨TD BGCOLOR=GREEN ALIGN=CENTER⟩Green⟨/TD⟩
　　⟨TD ALIGN=CENTER⟩⟨FONT FACE=COURIER SIZE=10⟩
　　Courier⟨/TD⟩
⟨/TR⟩
⟨/TABLE⟩

Figure 3.10
Creating a table in HTML

6 Your tags should now appear like those in Figure 3.10. Save your work as *Seventeen.html*.

⟨HTML⟩
⟨TITLE⟩HTML and JavaScript⟨/TITLE⟩

⟨BODY BGCOLOR=WHITE TEXT=BLUE LINK=RED
VLINK=GREEN⟩
⟨CENTER⟩⟨H1⟩Organizing Tags⟨/H1⟩⟨/CENTER⟩

⟨P⟩There are many ways to organize a Web page. This Web
page will organize text, hypertext links, colors, and fonts. It
will also demonstrate single spacing, double spacing, and the
use of line breaks.⟨/P⟩

⟨P⟩This Web page will display how to organize Web pages in
a number of ways using: ⟨/P⟩

⟨BR⟩⟨A HREF="#POWERFUL"⟩Powerful Lines⟨/A⟩
⟨BR⟩⟨A HREF="#HYPERLINKS"⟩Hyperlinks to HTML and
JavaScript sources⟨/A⟩
⟨BR⟩⟨A HREF="#PREVIOUS"⟩Hyperlinks to previously created
Web pages⟨/A⟩
⟨BR⟩⟨A HREF="#FONTS"⟩Fancy Fonts⟨/A⟩
⟨BR⟩⟨A HREF="#PICTURES"⟩Perfect Pictures⟨/A⟩
⟨BR⟩⟨**A HREF="#TABLES"**⟩Orderly Tables⟨/**A**⟩
⟨BR⟩Extraordinary Extras

⟨HR⟩
⟨P⟩⟨H2⟩⟨A NAME= "POWERFUL"⟩Powerful Lines⟨/A⟩⟨/H2⟩⟨/P⟩

A Horizontal Rule tag 50% wide and 10 increments high.
⟨HR WIDTH="50%" SIZE=10⟩

A Horizontal Rule tag 25% wide and 20 increments high.
⟨HR WIDTH="25%" SIZE=20⟩

A Horizontal Rule tag 10% wide and 30 increments high.
⟨HR WIDTH="10%" SIZE=30⟩

A Horizontal Rule tag without attributes and values.
⟨HR⟩

⟨P⟩⟨H2⟩⟨A NAME= "HYPERLINKS"⟩Hyperlinks
to HTML and JavaScript sources⟨/A⟩⟨/H2⟩⟨/P⟩

⟨BR⟩⟨A HREF="http://www.microsoft.com"⟩Microsoft⟨/A⟩
⟨BR⟩⟨A HREF="http://home.netscape.com"⟩Netscape⟨/A⟩
⟨BR⟩⟨A HREF="http://www.sun.com"⟩Sun Microsystems⟨/A⟩
⟨BR⟩⟨A HREF="http://www.oracle.com"⟩Oracle⟨/A⟩

⟨HR⟩
⟨P⟩⟨H2⟩⟨A NAME= "PREVIOUS"⟩ Hyperlinks to previously
created Web pages⟨/A⟩⟨/H2⟩⟨/P⟩

⟨BR⟩⟨A HREF="One.html"⟩One⟨/A⟩
⟨BR⟩⟨A HREF="Two.html"⟩Two⟨/A⟩
⟨BR⟩⟨A HREF="Three.html"⟩Three⟨/A⟩
⟨BR⟩⟨A HREF="Four.html"⟩Four⟨/A⟩
⟨BR⟩⟨A HREF="Five.html"⟩Five⟨/A⟩
⟨BR⟩⟨A HREF="Six.html"⟩Six⟨/A⟩
⟨BR⟩⟨A HREF="Seven.html"⟩Seven⟨/A⟩

⟨BR⟩⟨A HREF="Eight.html"⟩Eight⟨/A⟩
⟨BR⟩⟨A HREF="Nine.html"⟩Nine⟨/A⟩
⟨BR⟩⟨A HREF="Ten.html"⟩Ten⟨/A⟩
⟨BR⟩⟨A HREF="Eleven.html"⟩Eleven⟨/A⟩

⟨HR⟩
⟨P⟩⟨H2⟩⟨A NAME= "FONTS"⟩ Fancy Fonts ⟨/A⟩⟨/H2⟩⟨/P⟩

⟨BR⟩⟨FONT FACE=HELVETICA SIZE=4 COLOR=RED⟩This is
the Helvetica font at Size 4⟨/FONT⟩
⟨BR⟩⟨FONT FACE=TIMES SIZE=6 COLOR=GREEN⟩This is
the Times font at Size 6⟨/FONT⟩
⟨BR⟩⟨FONT FACE=ARIAL SIZE=8 COLOR=ORANGE⟩This is
the Arial font at Size 8⟨/FONT⟩
⟨BR⟩⟨FONT FACE=COURIER SIZE=2 COLOR=BLACK⟩This
is the Courier font at Size 2⟨/FONT⟩

⟨HR⟩
⟨P⟩⟨H2⟩⟨A NAME="PICTURES"⟩ Perfect Pictures ⟨/A⟩⟨/H2⟩⟨/P⟩

⟨P⟩⟨IMG SRC="levy.gif" ALIGN=RIGHT HEIGHT=50
Width=50⟩⟨/P⟩

⟨IMG SRC="levy.gif" HEIGHT=100 WIDTH=100⟩
⟨IMG SRC="levy.gif" HEIGHT=150 WIDTH=150⟩
⟨IMG SRC="levy.gif" HEIGHT=200 WIDTH=200⟩

⟨P⟩⟨IMG SRC="levy.gif" HEIGHT=150 WIDTH=150⟩⟨/P⟩
⟨P⟩⟨IMG SRC="levy.gif" HEIGHT=200 WIDTH=200⟩⟨/P⟩

⟨**HR**⟩
⟨**P**⟩⟨**H2**⟩⟨**A NAME= "TABLES"**⟩ **Orderly Tables** ⟨/**A**⟩⟨/**H2**⟩⟨/**P**⟩

⟨**TABLE BORDER=5 CELLPADDING=10 ALIGN=CENTER**⟩
⟨**TR**⟩
　　⟨**TH**⟩**Dragons**⟨/**TH**⟩
　　⟨**TH**⟩**Colors**⟨/**TH**⟩
　　⟨**TH**⟩**Fonts**⟨/**TH**⟩

These tags create the top row.

⟨/**TR**⟩
⟨**TR**⟩
　　⟨**TD**⟩⟨**IMG SRC="levy.gif" HEIGHT=50 WIDTH=50**⟩⟨/**TD**⟩
　　⟨**TD BGCOLOR=RED ALIGN=CENTER**⟩**Red**⟨/**TD**⟩
　　⟨**TD ALIGN=CENTER**⟩⟨**FONT FACE=TIMES SIZE=7
COLOR=GREEN**⟩**Times**⟨/**TD**⟩

These tags create the middle row.

⟨/**TR**⟩
⟨**TR**⟩
　　⟨**TD**⟩⟨**IMG SRC="levy.gif" HEIGHT=75 WIDTH=50**⟩⟨/**TD**⟩
　　⟨**TD BGCOLOR=GREEN ALIGN=CENTER**⟩**Green**⟨/**TD**⟩
　　⟨**TD ALIGN=CENTER**⟩⟨**FONT FACE=COURIER
SIZE=10**⟩**Courier**⟨/**TD**⟩

These tags create the bottom row.

⟨/**TR**⟩
⟨/**TABLE**⟩

⟨/BODY⟩
⟨/HTML⟩

---

7 View your work in your Web browser. Your new links should look like Figure 3.11. Test each link and make sure they all work. Make any corrections that are necessary.

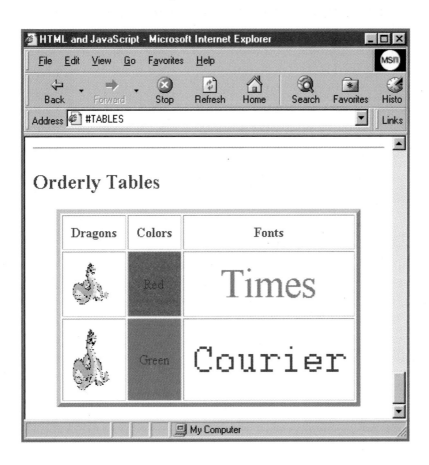

Figure 3.11
An HTML table as seen in your browser

THINKING ABOUT TECHNOLOGY

How can tables be used to display information? What kinds of things can you create with the table tags? How could you create a monthly calendar using HTML table tags? Give it a try. Create a calendar for this month. Save your work as *Calendar.html.* You can use this file later in another exercise.

Internet Milestone

Business on the Web

For many years, the Web was a tough place to make a living. The truth is, it took many years before the commercial potential of the Web was realized. Some of the first Web companies to start making a considerable profit online were America Online, Yahoo!, and Amazon.com.

Some succeeded online by daring to go where no one else dared to go. For many years, Internet users said that the Web would soon replace printed books. The people of Amazon.com took exception to that theory and began selling books on the Web. They sold so many books that other book companies realized that they must go online or give away a big portion of their business to Amazon.com. Barnes & Noble was one of the first major book sellers to join Amazon.com on the WWW.

Sony found out that the Web was a great place to sell music CDs. Egghead found the Web a great place to sell software. What other kinds of things can you think of that would become big sellers online? Can you set up a cyber-business and make lots of money from the Web?

ACTIVITY

3.5

Objective:
In this activity, you will add a variety of data input tags to your page.

Extraordinary Extras

In this activity, you will learn a few extra tags that add extraordinary power to your Web pages. These tags will allow those who visit your Web page to interact with the document.

There are many data input, or ⟨FORM⟩ tag, options that have been added to HTML. These options give you many ways to ask questions of visitors to your Web page. These tags give extra functionality to your Web page. These little "extras" can make your Web page more exciting and extraordinary.

There are four basic input tags you will enter. They include:

- Text boxes
- Drop down lists
- Radio buttons
- Checkboxes

This is the last activity before you jump into JavaScript. So, this will be a test of sorts. We will not give you all the tags to refer to. Think about how you should integrate the new tags into your Web page. Don't worry; you will pass with flying font colors. If you have any questions, review the steps in previous activities. Figure 3.12 displays the new tags you will be adding to your Web page.

Figure 3.12
A variety of data input tags

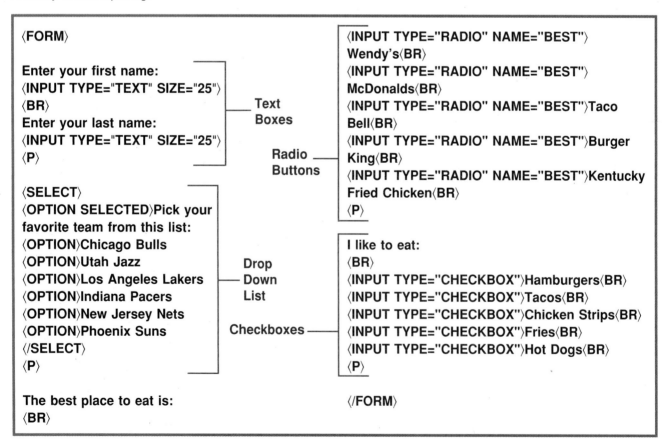

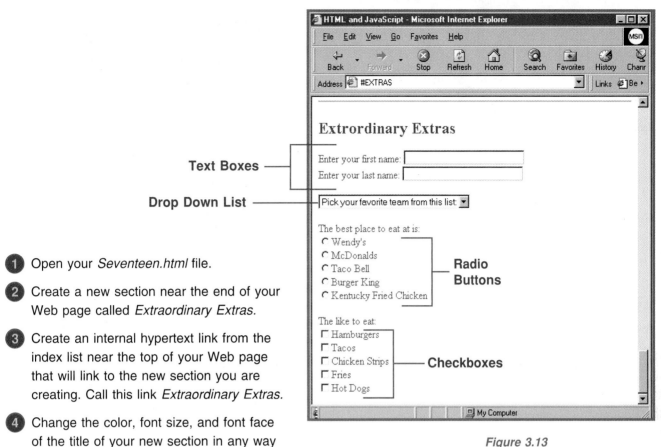

Text Boxes ——

Drop Down List ——

Figure 3.13
Extraordinary Extras created
with Forms

Radio Buttons

Checkboxes

1. Open your *Seventeen.html* file.

2. Create a new section near the end of your Web page called *Extraordinary Extras*.

3. Create an internal hypertext link from the index list near the top of your Web page that will link to the new section you are creating. Call this link *Extraordinary Extras*.

4. Change the color, font size, and font face of the title of your new section in any way you see fit.

5. Enter the tags shown in Figure 3.12 in your new Extraordinary Extras section, just before the ⟨/BODY⟩ tag at the bottom of the page.

6. Save your work as *Eighteen.html*.

7. Open your Web browser and try all the input options. They should appear like those found in Figure 3.13. Which ones work? Correct any errors you find, resave, and try them again.

8. Make your own form. Return to your Web page and change all the selection items.

9. Save your work as *Eighteen-2.html* and test your changes. How did they work?

THINKING ABOUT TECHNOLOGY

Each of these extraordinary input boxes asks the user to supply a different kind of information. What kinds of responses would you expect from the following FORM attributes?

TEXT
OPTION
RADIO
CHECKBOX

Downloading Too Many Pictures

It is considered impolite to download pictures to your school network that you don't intend to use. Graphics take up a great deal of space on a computer. Downloading hundreds and hundreds of pictures and not using them is a waste of network server drive space. Consider deleting any pictures you aren't actually using.

NET VOCABULARY

Define the following terms:

1. .gif

2. .jpg or .jpeg

3. fonts

4. graphics

5. Graphics Interchange Format

6. image

7. Joint Photographic Expert Group

8. table cell

NET REVIEW

Give a short answer to the following questions:

1. Why are artists in such demand on the WWW?

2. When is it illegal to take pictures off the Web?

3. Why is it important not to download pictures to your school or workplace network if you do not plan to use them?

4. How and why would you use the following tags?

    〈B〉〈/B〉

⟨EM⟩⟨/EM⟩

⟨STRONG⟩⟨/STRONG⟩

⟨I⟩⟨/I⟩

5. How and why would you use the BACKGROUND attribute?

6. What tags would you use to make a graphic a hyperlink?

CREATING AN ONLINE SURVEY

Great Applications, Inc. wants to enter the online video game business. However, before it starts programming the next great online video game, it wants to survey potential customers to see what kinds of online games they want to play and buy.

Brainstorm 10 questions that will help Great Applications learn what its customers want in a video game program. Use your ⟨FORM⟩ tag skills, and create an online survey to gather information from potential customers. Have your survey ask for the respondent's name and email address. Ask questions that utilize drop down lists, radio selection items, and checkboxes.

NET PROJECT TEAMWORK   A Table Tour

Great Applications, Inc. is asking your team to plan a world tour to demonstrate its new software video games to people in five major cities. You and your team have been asked to create a calendar of events for the tour using ⟨TABLE⟩ tags. The tour must be conducted during a single month and should involve five major cities.

When you create your calendar, create links to tourist information about the cities that you will be visiting on the tour. Use cell padding and cell borders to make the table interesting. You can even put pictures in the cells to illustrate the five cities you have selected for the software rollout.

To save some time, borrow the calendar you created in the *Thinking About Technology* section in Activity 3.4. Modify these tags to fit this exercise.

WRITING ABOUT TECHNOLOGY

Before you complete this section on HTML and move on to JavaScript, evaluate the impact and importance of HTML on worldwide communications and the economy.

How important is the WWW and HTML to the world's economy?

_____

_____

_____

_____

_____

How does the Web benefit small businesses around the world?

_____

_____

_____

_____

Over 500 years ago, Gutenberg created the printing press and changed the history of the world. Five hundred years from now, how will people look back on the invention of HTML?

_____

_____

_____

_____

_____

What extra features or tags would you like to see added to HTML? Are there any tags that you think should be added to give more power to HTML?

_____

_____

_____

_____

_____

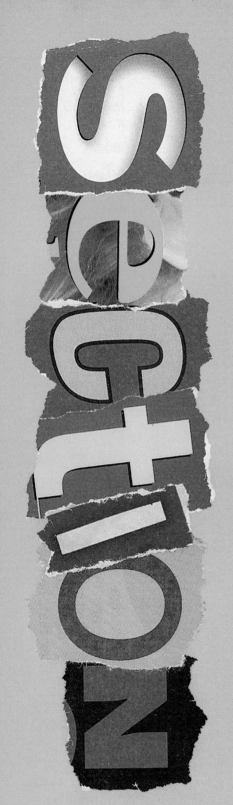

The Exciting World of JavaScript

Welcome to the exciting world of JavaScript! In the previous three chapters, you learned the fundamentals of creating Web pages with HyperText Markup Language (HTML), but now it is time to move into a different realm of Internet development.

HTML is a powerful tool in many respects, and it is capable of doing a lot of interesting things on the Web. In fact, more than any other technology, HTML is responsible for the tremendous popularity of the Internet today. Nevertheless, it is still a fact that HTML has its limitations. There simply are a lot of Internet programming tasks that cannot be accomplished with HTML, so it did not take long for professional software developers to start demanding something more. As a result, there are now several different Internet technologies available that were developed by several different companies. It is likely that you have heard of some of these products, such as CGI, PERL, CORBA, Java, and of course, JavaScript. Each of these technologies was designed to address different programming needs, so professional programmers tend to choose different tools to solve different problems. But they all have one thing in common, and that is that they all rely on HTML in some way to move around through cyberspace.

You could say that the HyperText Transport Protocol (HTTP) is the information superhighway, and HTML represents the various "vehicles" that travel on the superhighway. These vehicles come in numerous shapes and sizes, and they carry different types of payloads, but they all have a common bond.

Now you understand the HTML foundation of the Internet, and that JavaScript was designed to enhance that foundation. It probably won't surprise you to learn that the way in which Web page developers embed JavaScript code into their HTML documents is by using two special tags:

⟨SCRIPT⟩ ⟨/SCRIPT⟩

These tags inform the Web browser that the text that appears between these tags is to be interpreted as part of a JavaScript program, rather than as literal information to be displayed on the screen. This is where JavaScript begins to move you into the world of *programming* and away from the world of *formatting*. Unlike a true programming language, however, JavaScript does not require you to go out and purchase a specialized software package in order to convert it from its human-readable form (called *source code*) into a machine-readable form (called *object code, binary code, executable code,* or *machine code*). Traditional programming languages such as Pascal, C++, or even Java perform the conversion by means of a *compiler,* and they usually come with a specialized editor, debugger, project manager, online help system, etc. These types of software packages are known as Integrated Development Environments (IDEs), and some of them are very expensive! But with JavaScript, you can create your source code in exactly the same way you create HTML code— with a simple text editor or word processor. When the HTML document, with its embedded JavaScript program, is loaded by a browser, the program is converted into machine code and executed. Its *output* is displayed as part of the resulting HTML document. In other words, it is entirely possible that a single Web page document could display something entirely different on one computer system than it does on another. It could even display something entirely different one minute than it did on the same computer system the minute before! We'll learn more about this in Chapter 4.

JavaScript gives you many of the capabilities of a full-fledged programming language while maintaining the simplicity of HTML coding. Now that's a useful and effective combination!

Hopefully this brief introduction to JavaScript has peaked your interest, so let's get busy learning more about what it is, what it can do, and how it does it.

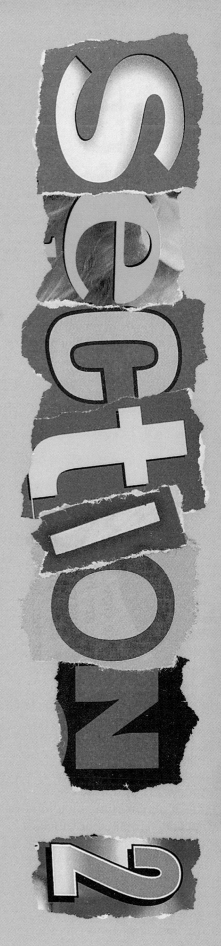

What Is JavaScript?

Chapter Objectives

In this chapter, you will be introduced to JavaScript. After reading Chapter 4, you will be able to

1 understand the purpose of JavaScript.

2 use the ⟨SCRIPT⟩ and ⟨/SCRIPT⟩ tags.

3 learn to use JavaScript objects.

4 learn to use JavaScript methods.

5 understand JavaScript syntax.

JavaScript Terms

binary code

compiler

condition

interpretation

keywords

methods

objects

operators

parameter list

programming language

scripting language

⟨SCRIPT⟩ and ⟨/SCRIPT⟩ tags

status line

syntax

token

Web browser

An Introduction to JavaScript

JavaScript is sometimes referred to as a **programming language,** but it is really more accurate to call it a **scripting language.** The difference between a programming language and a scripting language is fairly subtle but important to understand. Both types of languages must be converted from a human-readable form into a machine-readable form. For programming languages, this process is performed *before* the program runs, by a highly specialized piece of software called a **compiler.** The programmer is not only aware than this conversion must happen but also is in control of the operation. With a scripting language, however, there is no need to explicitly invoke the code conversion process. It happens automatically in the background when the source code is processed by the target program. To be more specific, an HTML document must be written by a human and then processed by a special type of program called a **Web browser.** And when that HTML document contains embedded JavaScript code, that code is *interpreted* by the Web browser, and converted into a machine-readable format "on-the-fly." **Interpretation** is simply the term programmers use to describe this line-by-line conversion process that occurs automatically at run time.

Under normal conditions, the output of the JavaScript

code will be nothing more than a string (or perhaps many strings) of text that are simply inserted into the HTML page. The resulting page is displayed by a Web browser just as it would be if that resulting text had been typed into the original HTML source document by a human. The real power of embedding JavaScript into HTML documents comes from the fact that the resulting text described above can change from one day to the next, or even from one minute to the next. It is entirely possible for one person to enter a particular URL into his Web browser and see a Web page that is completely different from that seen by another person who enters the exact same URL! These differences could be due to differences in time, differences in location, or even differences in Web browsers. JavaScript is capable of detecting various conditions in the current operating environment and reacting accordingly. This concept is explored in greater detail in Activity 4.3.

It is extremely easy for a Web browser to detect if a particular HTML page contains embedded JavaScript code or not. All that is required is for the person creating the document to use the ⟨SCRIPT⟩ tag to mark the beginning of a JavaScript section and then use the ⟨/SCRIPT⟩ tag to indicate the end of that section. Everything between these two tags will be interpreted by the Web browser as JavaScript source code rather than standard HTML text. The browser will then convert the script (via the interpretation process) into its equivalent machine-readable form called **binary code.** This binary code will then be executed, and its output (if any) will be inserted into the HTML text stream and displayed as if it has been typed into the original HTML document by a human. Are you following?

It is also important for you to understand that the scripts you will be embedding between the ⟨SCRIPT⟩ and ⟨/SCRIPT⟩ tags cannot be any old text you care to put in there. On the contrary, the text must conform to some fairly rigid rules, or the Web browser will display a nasty error message on the screen when you try to view your page. This is precisely why JavaScript is called a scripting *language*—because it must adhere to precise rules of grammar known as program **syntax.** In this chapter, you will learn about JavaScript objects and methods, as well as JavaScript keywords and operators. Once you have these basic programming elements under control, you will be able to start building big, sophisticated scripts in no time.

Enough of the preliminaries—let's get to work! ■

NET FACT

Which Came First—Java or JavaScript?

Many people who have only a casual knowledge of Internet technologies tend to think that Java programming language and JavaScript scripting language are the same thing. Even those who know that they are *not* the same thing sometimes wonder how they relate to each other or which one was created first. The answer is that Java was created first by Sun Microsystems, Inc. Sun released its new cross-platform programming language to the general public in 1995, and it has continued to grow in popularity at an unprecedented rate ever since.

Sun was not the only company looking for a way to enhance the capabilities of standard HTML. Netscape Communications Corporation also had been busy working on a way to embed programmable scripts into HTML Web pages, and they needed to incorporate a well-defined syntax into their design. When the Netscape developers saw how popular Java language was becoming, they decided to license the Java name from Sun and use the Java syntax in their own scripting language. The end result of Netscape's efforts was JavaScript, and they have enjoyed a considerable amount of success with this technology as well.

ACTIVITY

4.1

Objective:

In this activity, you will learn to use the write() method of the document object.

Hello World Wide Web!

The primary purpose of JavaScript code is to generate text that will be inserted into the standard HTML text stream. JavaScript is essentially made up of a number of invisible entities, called **objects,** that contain a well-defined set of capabilities. In order for JavaScript programmers to make use of these capabilities, they must call upon the services of one or more specialized functions, known as **methods,** within those objects. The way in which a method is invoked is for the programmer to type in the name of the object, followed by a period (the . character), followed by the method name.

Method names are always followed by a **parameter list,** even though there are sometimes no items in the list. Perhaps the best way to understand method parameters is to visualize a list of ingredients for a recipe. The parameter list simply provides the method with the information it needs to perform its specific function correctly. The syntax of a parameter list consists of an opening parenthesis [( ], zero or more parameter items (separated by commas), and a closing parenthesis [ )]. For example, if you wanted to invoke the write() method of the JavaScript document object, you would do so like this:

```
document.write("A string of text")
```

Now that you've seen a simple example of JavaScript coding, let's give you a chance to incorporate this example into an actual HTML document that contains embedded JavaScript. Are you ready? Then let's do it.

1 Open your text editor or word processor, and type the HTML/JavaScript code exactly as it appears in Figure 4.1. (See *Netiquette: Mind Your Braces,* p. 89, for information on why some of the text in Figure 4.1 is indented.)

```
⟨HTML⟩
⟨HEAD⟩
⟨TITLE⟩JavaScript Activity #1⟨/TITLE⟩
⟨/HEAD⟩
⟨BODY⟩
⟨SCRIPT⟩
      document.write("Hello World Wide Web!");
⟨/SCRIPT⟩
⟨/BODY⟩
⟨/HTML⟩
```

Figure 4.1
HTML and JavaScript code

2 Save this file in the appropriate folder as *js-one.html.*

3 Open your Web browser.

4 View your *js-one.html* page. You should see an image that looks like Figure 4.2. (Refer back to Activity 1.3 if you need a reminder on how to view an .html file in your Web browser.)

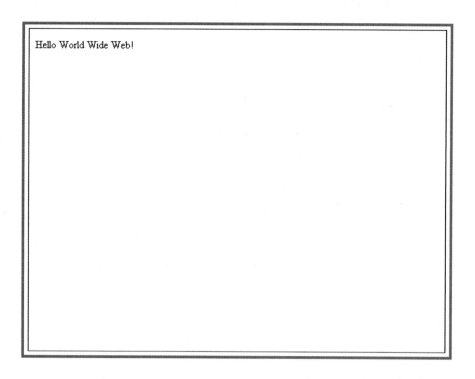

Hello World Wide Web!

Figure 4.2
Your first page created with JavaScript

At this point, you may be thinking that this Web page doesn't look all that impressive. If so, you are absolutely correct! But don't give up on JavaScript yet, because we are just getting started. By the time you have worked through a few more activities, you will start to see that JavaScript is capable of much more than this simplistic Web page demonstrates.

The main point is that you have now written one line of JavaScript code, and it actually worked! That should be worth something, right?

THINKING ABOUT TECHNOLOGY

Hopefully you will recognize the fact that there is nothing special about the phrase "Hello World Wide Web!" is this exercise. This phrase could be replaced with any other string of text, and the JavaScript code would still work just fine. The only thing you have to keep in mind is that the text you want displayed must appear between the opening and closing double quote characters ("). Try changing the message in the write() method to make sure you understand what is really happening here. Try typing in a very long string of text, and then see how the Web browser formats the text on the screen. Also, try inserting several document.write() statements and see how the browser handles them. You might be surprised!

ACTIVITY

4.2

Objective:

In this activity, you will learn how JavaScript interacts with HTML.

Enhancing the Appearance of Your Web Page

As we have mentioned earlier in this chapter, the JavaScript method called *document.write()* simply inserts a string of characters into the standard HTML text stream. Another way to think of it is that after the browser has finished processing the HTML document, the effective result is that the ⟨SCRIPT⟩ tag, the ⟨/SCRIPT⟩ tag, and everything in between the two will be stripped out of the page and replaced by whatever string appears as the parameter of the write() method. This means that any HTML formatting tags we may put before or after the script will be processed just like they would be in a Web page without any embedded JavaScript code. To illustrate this point more clearly, let's modify the Web page we created in Activity 4.1. Let's add some HTML formatting codes so that our "Hello World Wide Web!" message looks a little more appealing on the screen. Let's also add a second message to the page to make sure you are understanding the interaction between HTML and JavaScript.

1. Open your text editor or word processor and retrieve the *js-one.html* file you created in the previous activity.

2. Change the activity number to 2.

3. Next, you're going to make the text you just created with JavaScript an ⟨H1⟩ heading, and you'll create a new ⟨H3⟩ heading with more Java-Script. You'll also want to center both headings. To do all of this, inside the ⟨BODY⟩ and ⟨/BODY⟩ tags, add the ⟨CENTER⟩⟨/CENTER⟩ tags, the ⟨H1⟩⟨/H1⟩ tags, the ⟨H3⟩⟨/H3⟩ tags, and a new line of JavaScript, as shown in bold at the top of page 79 and in Figure 4.3.

```
⟨HTML⟩
⟨HEAD⟩
⟨TITLE⟩JavaScript Activity #2⟨/TITLE⟩
⟨/HEAD⟩
⟨BODY⟩
⟨CENTER⟩
⟨H1⟩
⟨SCRIPT⟩
    document.write("Hello World Wide Web!");
⟨/SCRIPT⟩
⟨/H1⟩
⟨H3⟩
⟨SCRIPT⟩
    document.write("Welcome to the exciting world of JavaScript.");
⟨/SCRIPT⟩
⟨/H3⟩
⟨/CENTER⟩
⟨/BODY⟩
⟨/HTML⟩
```

Figure 4.3
JavaScript Web page containing HTML formatting tags

```
⟨BODY⟩
⟨CENTER⟩
⟨H1⟩
⟨SCRIPT⟩
     document.write("Hello World Wide Web!");
⟨/SCRIPT⟩
⟨/H1⟩
⟨H3⟩
⟨SCRIPT⟩
     document.write("Welcome to the exciting world of JavaScript.");
⟨/SCRIPT⟩
⟨/H3⟩
⟨/CENTER⟩
```

4 Your new file should look like Figure 4.3.

5 Save your new file as *js-two.html.*

6 Open your Web browser and view your *js-two.html* file. Your page should look just like Figure 4.4.

Hello World Wide Web!

Welcome to the exciting world of JavaScript.

Figure 4.4
A nicely formatted JavaScript Web page

If you attained a clear understanding of the HTML material presented in Chapter 1, you should be comfortable with the purpose of the center and heading tags we added to this document. You should also understand that the output string that comes from the first call to (or occurrence of) the document.write() method will be inserted into the HTML text stream between the ⟨CENTER⟩ and ⟨/CENTER⟩ tags, as well as between the ⟨H1⟩⟨/H1⟩ tags. Likewise, the output string produced by the second call to (occurrence of) document.write() will also appear between the ⟨CENTER⟩⟨/CENTER⟩ tags, in addition to the ⟨H3⟩⟨/H3⟩ tags. In other words, the ⟨H1⟩⟨/H1⟩ tags will only affect the appearance of the first output string, and the ⟨H3⟩⟨/H3⟩ tags will only affect the second string. But the ⟨CENTER⟩⟨/CENTER⟩ tags will affect the position of both output strings. Got it?

WARNING: You may be tempted to place HTML formatting tags (such as ⟨CENTER⟩ or ⟨H1⟩) around the document.write() statement, rather than outside of the ⟨SCRIPT⟩ and ⟨/SCRIPT⟩ tags. Don't do it! You need to remember that everything you type between the script tags will be interpreted by the Web browser as JavaScript code, and misplaced HTML tags do not conform to the rules of JavaScript syntax. Even though it is possible to embed HTML tags in JavaScript output (as shown in the next activity), these tags cannot be placed around JavaScript statements. If you try it, the result will be an error message from your browser.

THINKING ABOUT TECHNOLOGY

It should be clear to you that you can use any HTML tags with JavaScript, not just the heading and center tags. Try inserting some of the other HTML tags described in the first three chapters into this activity to see what effect they will have. Specifically, try using the tags that affect the foreground and background colors of the Web page. See if you can get your JavaScript Web page to appear as yellow text on a blue background, for example. Or try to make the ⟨H1⟩ text appear in a different color than the ⟨H3⟩ text. You can do that, right?

NET TIP

What's with Those Troublesome Semicolons?

If you were to study the source code for many different JavaScript-enabled Web pages on the Internet, you would discover that many of them have semicolons (;) after each statement, while many others do not. All of the source listings for the JavaScript activities in this chapter include semicolons, but they are not necessary. If you were to go through each activity one by one and remove the terminating semicolons, all of the scripts would still function correctly. So you may be asking yourself why they are there. The answer is that it is a matter of personal preference—at least in these examples. But if you were to move from Java-Script coding to some other programming languages (including Pascal, C++, and Java), you would find that the semicolons are no longer optional. Each of these languages will display an error message if you forget to put in a required semicolon, so we feel that it's a good idea to get used to them. After all, it is usually much easier to learn a good habit than to unlearn a bad one, right?

Conditional Statements in JavaScript

Objective:
In this activity, you should acquire an understanding of what conditional statements are and how they are implemented in JavaScript.

The astute student may look at the previous two activities and ask, "Why are we even using JavaScript to display text messages on the screen? Wouldn't it be easier to just type the text into the HTML document and eliminate the calls to the document.write() method?" Well, the honest answer is "Yes!" It would be easier to do it that way. In fact, the Web browser would even display the results slightly faster if we eliminated the script tags because it wouldn't have to invoke the JavaScript interpreter. However, don't forget that JavaScript is capable of performing a lot more functions than simply writing text to the screen. In this activity, you will use one of the most powerful features of the JavaScript language, the *conditional statement*. Every programming language possesses the ability to make decisions. Or to put it in more technical terms, every language gives programmers the ability to evaluate a specific condition and then perform different actions depending on the results of that evaluation.

The syntax of the conditional statement in JavaScript is very important. The statement begins with the keyword *if,* and then a condition is specified within a pair of parentheses. A **keyword** is recognized as part of the language definition. It is reserved by the language and cannot be used as a variable. Some examples of keywords are *if, else,* and *return.*

The condition is followed by a *statement block* which consists of an opening brace ({), one or more JavaScript statements, and then a closing brace (}). The shell of a JavaScript conditional statement is shown in Figure 4.5.

```
if (〈condition〉)
{
    statement 1;
    statement 2;
    statement 3;
        .
        .
        .
    statement N;
}
```

Figure 4.5
JavaScript conditional statement shell

Internet Milestone

The Beginning of Scripting

When Netscape Communications Corporation introduced JavaScript to the world in 1995, they were not the first company to provide Web content developers with a new technology to enhance the capabilities of HTML. However, they were the first to provide a full-featured scripting language, and it didn't take long for other companies to recognize the advantages of this technology.

While scripting does not provide all of the features of a complete programming language, it also does not require the use of complex or expensive compiler software. This makes it an ideal choice for novice programmers, educational institutions, or other organizations with limited financial resources.

So in 1996, Microsoft Corporation quickly joined the scripting bandwagon by offering both JScript and VBScript as alternatives to the industry-standard JavaScript. These scripting languages are roughly equivalent to JavaScript in terms of the capabilities they provide, but they also offer a few extra features to those users who run Microsoft's Internet Explorer on the Windows platform. Like JavaScript, JScript is based on the syntax of the Java programming language, while VBScript is based on the programming syntax of Visual Basic.

The scripting language of choice for professional developers depends upon their particular preferences and programming needs. But no matter which language they choose, they can thank JavaScript for getting the scripting movement started.

```
if (⟨condition⟩)
{
    statement i1;
    statement i2;
    statement i3;
         .
         .
         .
    statement iN;
}
else
{
    statement e1;
    statement e2;
    statement e3;
         .
         .
         .
    statement eN;
}
```

Figure 4.6
JavaScript conditional statement
shell with *else* clause

The JavaScript *if* statement also supports an optional *else* clause, which defines the action to take if the specified condition is not true. The *else* keyword appears immediately after the statement block of the *if* clause, and it contains a statement block of its own. An example of a JavaScript conditional statement that includes the optional *else* clause is shown in Figure 4.6.

Now that you know the basic structure of JavaScript *if* and *if-else* statements, let's talk a little about the **condition** part of the syntax (shown as ⟨*condition*⟩ in Figures 4.5 and 4.6). A JavaScript condition will always consist of two **tokens** separated by a relational **operator.** A token can be either a variable name (such as *x* or *count*) or a literal constant (such as *10* or *Shane*). The relational operator may be any one of the following:

Operator	Meaning
==	is equal to
!=	is not equal to
⟨	is less than
⟩	is greater than
⟨=	is less than or equal to
⟩=	is greater than or equal to

NOTE: Make sure that you use two equal sign characters (= =) when testing for equality. If you forget and use only one equal sign, your Web browser will reprimand you with an error message!

Now that you have learned how to create conditional statements in JavaScript, let's put that knowledge to work in an actual program. In this activity, we will include a simple conditional statement, and teach you a useful programming technique in the process. It is fairly common for Web page developers to want to perform different tasks, depending on the type of browser a particular user has. The JavaScript program you are about to create will determine if the Web surfer is using Netscape Navigator or not, and then it will react accordingly. Check it out!

1 Open your text editor or word processor, and retrieve the *js-two.html* file.

2 Change the activity number to 3.

3 Just after the closing ⟨/H3⟩ tag but before the closing ⟨/CENTER⟩ tag, enter a new JavaScript statement, as shown in bold here and in Figure 4.7.

```
⟨/H3⟩
⟨SCRIPT⟩
    if (navigator.appName == "Netscape")
    {
        document.write("You are using Netscape Navigator.");
    }
    else
    {
        document.write("You are not using Netscape Navigator.⟨BR⟩");
```

```
        document.write("I'll bet you're using Internet Explorer.");
    }
⟨/SCRIPT⟩
⟨/CENTER⟩
```

④ Your completed file should look like Figure 4.7.

```
⟨HTML⟩
⟨HEAD⟩
⟨TITLE⟩JavaScript Activity #3⟨/TITLE⟩
⟨/HEAD⟩
⟨BODY⟩
⟨CENTER⟩
⟨H1⟩
⟨SCRIPT⟩
    document.write("Hello World Wide Web!");
⟨/SCRIPT⟩
⟨/H1⟩
⟨H3⟩
⟨SCRIPT⟩
    document.write("Welcome to the exciting world of JavaScript.");
⟨/SCRIPT⟩
⟨/H3⟩
⟨SCRIPT⟩
    if (navigator.appName == "Netscape")
    {
        document.write("You are using Netscape Navigator.");
    }
    else
    {
        document.write("You are not using Netscape Navigator.⟨BR⟩");
        document.write("I'll bet you're using Internet Explorer.");
    }
⟨/SCRIPT⟩
⟨/CENTER⟩
⟨/BODY⟩
⟨/HTML⟩
```

Figure 4.7
HTML/JavaScript
document with *if-else*
conditional statement

Net Fun

If you would like to check out a fun demo of what JavaScript can do, fire up your browser and go to *http://www. javascript.com*. This site contains a cyberspace version of the mystical 8-ball toy with which many of us are familiar. The object of the toy is to provide an answer to any question you wish to ask it. Well, here is a Web site that can do the same thing for you!

5 After you have completed your edits, save the resulting file with the name *js-three.html.*

6 Start your Web browser, and load the *js-three.html* file, as you did in the previous two activities. If you are using Netscape Navigator, your screen should now look like Figure 4.8a. But if you are not using Netscape Navigator, your screen should look like Figure 4.8b.

Hello World Wide Web!

Welcome to the exciting world of JavaScript.

You are using Netscape Navigator.

Figure 4.8a
Resulting Web page when using Netscape Navigator

Hello World Wide Web!

Welcome to the exciting world of JavaScript.

You are not using Netscape Navigator.
I'll bet you're using Internet Explorer.

Figure 4.8b
Resulting Web Page when not using Netscape Navigator

Chapter 4 What Is JavaScript?

Even though we didn't add a whole lot of code to our JavaScript program, we did introduce several important concepts. Let's take a minute to review those concepts to make sure you have a solid understanding of what is happening here.

First of all, the condition being evaluated in this JavaScript program is:

(navigator.appName == "Netscape")

We mentioned earlier in this chapter that JavaScript objects contain special functions, called methods, that perform various tasks. Well, it just so happens that JavaScript objects also contain *properties* that programmers can access to obtain information about the object. In this case, we are utilizing the appName property of the navigator object in order to determine the application name of the current Web browser. (Please note that in this context, the word "navigator" can be used interchangeably with the word "browser.") If this name is "Netscape," then we know the user is running Netscape Navigator. Otherwise, we know the user is not running Netscape Navigator, so he or she probably is running Microsoft's Internet Explorer (although there is a small chance it could be some other browser).

The second important concept to learn here is that once the condition has been evaluated, either the *if* statement block will be executed *or* the *else* block will be executed—never both. If the result of the condition is true, the if block will run. If the condition is false, the else block will run. It's as simple as that.

There is a final point in this example we would like you to recognize. Until now, we have repeatedly mentioned the concept of embedding JavaScript source code in HTML documents. Well, it turns out that it is also possible, not to mention useful, to embed HTML tags in JavaScript text strings! Look carefully at the first call to document.write() inside the *else* statement block. Notice that the HTML ⟨BR⟩ tag is embedded within the output text string. The reason this tag is present is because we wanted the second string of text to appear on a separate line, rather than on the same line as the first string. In order to accomplish this, we have to put a ⟨BR⟩ tag in the output text stream so that the browser will recognize the BREAK command. Are you still with us? Good.

THINKING ABOUT TECHNOLOGY

Do you suppose that ⟨BR⟩ is the only HTML formatting tag that can be embedded in a JavaScript output string? Of course it isn't. You can use any formatting tags you wish in a document.write() parameter string. Try being creative for a moment, and see how many other tags you can put in the JavaScript code for this activity. What effect, if any, do they have on the resulting Web page? Is it better to place HTML tags outside of the script tags, or is it better to embed them in JavaScript text strings? Are there times when you might want to do both? Think about it!

ACTIVITY
4.4

Objective:
In this activity, you will learn how to use the JavaScript alert() method.

Using the JavaScript Alert( ) Method

In the previous three activities, we have made use of the document.write() method, which is probably the most common way for JavaScript programs to communicate with the user. However, there are other ways in which scripts can get the user's attention. One such way is by means of the JavaScript *alert()* method. The purpose of the alert() method is to allow the program to display a special dialog box that will alert the user that an expected event has occurred, or that some kind of user input is required. Unlike the write() method or the appName property, the alert() method is not part of an object. Instead, this method is part of the JavaScript interpreter itself, and it interacts directly with the underlying operating system. (A detailed description of what an operating system is and what functions it performs is beyond the scope of this book. However, the operating system is Microsoft Windows on most PCs, MacOS on Macintosh computers, UNIX on some workstations, etc.) For this reason, it is not necessary to include an object name and a period (.) character when it is invoked. Let's give it a try, shall we?

1. Open your text editor or word processor like before, and retrieve the *js-three.html* file.

2. Change the activity number located between the TITLE tags to 4.

3. Add an alert statement to the *if* block, as shown in bold on p. 87 and in Figure 4.9.

NET TIP

To Space or Not to Space

If you look closely at the source code listing of Figure 4.7, you will see that there is a space between the if *keyword and the opening parenthesis of the condition. You will also see that there is no space between the* write *method name and the opening parenthesis of its parameter list. Although this may seem inconsistent at first, it is the way that most professional programmers would do it.*

As far as the JavaScript interpreter is concerned, the space is optional in both cases. You may put a space in or leave it out, and the script will still function correctly. However, there is a distinct syntactical difference between a JavaScript statement *and a JavaScript* method call. *A JavaScript statement will always contain one or more keywords, and it is customary to place "white space" around keywords. On the other hand, every JavaScript method name must be accompanied by a parameter list, so it is preferable to not put a space between the name and its parameters.*

Following these two programming style conventions will help make your JavaScript code much more readable by other programmers. You may have to think about it a little at first, but it will soon become second nature.

```
    {
        document.write("You are using Netscape Navigator.");
        alert("Netscape Navigator detected.");
    }
```

4 Add a second alert statement to the *else* block, as shown in bold here and in Figure 4.9.

```
    {
        document.write("You are not using Netscape Navigator.⟨BR⟩");
        document.write("I'll bet you're using Internet Explorer.");
        alert("Netscape Navigator required.");
    }
```

5 When you have made the necessary changes to the HTML document, save it with the new file name *js-four.html*.

```
⟨HTML⟩
⟨HEAD⟩
⟨TITLE⟩JavaScript Activity #4⟨/TITLE⟩
⟨/HEAD⟩
⟨BODY⟩
⟨CENTER⟩
⟨H1⟩
⟨SCRIPT⟩
    document.write("Hello World Wide Web!");
⟨/SCRIPT⟩
⟨/H1⟩
⟨H3⟩
⟨SCRIPT⟩
    document.write("Welcome to the exciting world of JavaScript.");
⟨/SCRIPT⟩
⟨/H3⟩
⟨SCRIPT⟩
    if (navigator.appName == "Netscape")
    {
        document.write("You are using Netscape Navigator.");
        alert("Netscape Navigator detected.");
    }
    else
    {
        document.write("You are not using Netscape Navigator.⟨BR⟩");
        document.write("I'll bet you're using Internet Explorer.");
        alert("Netscape Navigator required.");
    }
⟨/SCRIPT⟩
⟨/CENTER⟩
⟨/BODY⟩
⟨/HTML⟩
```

Figure 4.9
JavaScript source code containing calls to the *alert()* method

6 Open your Web browser and view your *js-four.html* file. If you are running Netscape Navigator, your screen should look like Figure 4.10a. But if you are running Microsoft's Internet Explorer, your screen will look like Figure 4.10b.

Hopefully this activity has helped you to see how the alert() method could be useful in some situations. It normally is used in JavaScript programs when the user needs to be made aware that

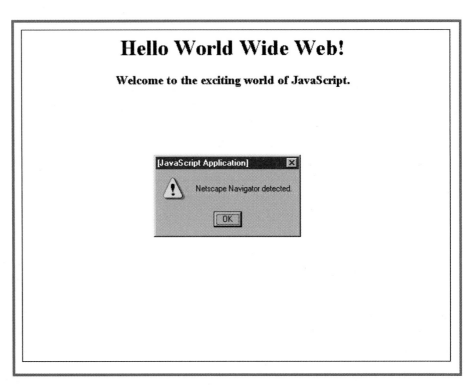

Figure 4.10a
Your screen in Netscape Navigator

Figure 4.10b
Your screen in Internet Explorer

some unexpected error condition has occurred. It can also be used, however, if the program needs some kind of user acknowledgement before proceeding. In either case, the alert() method is an alternative way for JavaScript software to generate output.

THINKING ABOUT TECHNOLOGY

In this activity, we have demonstrated how to define a conditional statement that evaluates the contents of the navigator.appName property to determine if it contains the value "Netscape." But if the appName property does not contain the value "Netscape," what value does it contain? How can you find out? Well, think about the document.write() method for a minute. Can it be used to display more than just a literal string (in double quotes)? Of course it can. It can also be used to display the contents of a JavaScript variable or an object property. Now you can write a JavaScript statement that displays the value of appName, can't you? Sure you can. Try it!

Mind Your Braces!

One of the characteristics of the JavaScript language that novice programmers tend to struggle with is the use of "curly braces." The opening brace ({) indicates the beginning of a statement block, and the closing brace (}) marks the end of that block.

Although the rules of JavaScript syntax are somewhat flexible when it comes to the placement of these braces, we strongly recommend that you follow the style shown in this book. If you start getting sloppy or inconsistent with the way you place your braces, it is very easy to cause yourself some serious problems. When the number of opening braces does not correspond to the number of closing braces, your Web browser will report a syntax error. However, it is also possible for braces to be placed in such a way that no syntax error occurs, but the program still will not run correctly.

The bottom line is that you can save yourself a lot of headaches by following a few simple rules:

1. Always place the opening brace directly below the keyword to which it belongs.
2. Always indent the statements contained within the statement block.
3. Always place the closing brace so that it is vertically aligned with its corresponding open brace.

If you remember to follow these rules, it becomes very easy to see what statements are contained within a particular statement block and to what keyword the block belongs. Never forget that it is often necessary for someone else to read your code, and this becomes a difficult task when statement blocks are disorganized or carelessly defined. It is simply a matter of professional courtesy to write legible code that is formatted logically and indented consistently. So please be considerate!

ACTIVITY
4.5

Objective:
In this activity, you will learn
how to display messages
in the status line of your
Web browser.

Accessing the Browser Status Line

You have probably noticed that when your Web browser is loading an HTML document that contains many objects, it displays various messages at the bottom of the window. This area of the screen is known as the **status line,** and it can be accessed from within a JavaScript program. In addition to the document.write() method and the alert() method, this is another way in which a JavaScript Web page can communicate information to the user.

The question you should be asking yourself now is, "How do I access the browser status line?" Once again, the answer to this question is very simple. The message displayed in the status line is nothing more than a string value that is stored in the *status* property of the *window* object. This means you can change the message at any time within a JavaScript program by including a statement like this:

```
window.status = "A string of text";
```

Now that you understand how easy it can be, let's add two new lines of code to the JavaScript program you wrote in the previous activity. This code will simply reinforce the messages that are displayed by the alert() method.

1. Open your text editor or word processor like before, and retrieve the *js-four.html* file.

2. Change the activity number located between the title tags to 5.

3. Add a window status statement to the *if* block, as shown in bold here and in Figure 4.11.

```
{
    document.write("You are using Netscape Navigator.");
    window.status = "Netscape Navigator detected.";
    alert("Netscape Navigator detected.");
}
```

4. Add a second window status statement to the *else* block, as shown in bold here and in Figure 4.11.

```
{
    document.write("You are not using Netscape Navigator.⟨BR⟩");
    document.write("I'll bet you're using Internet Explorer.");
    window.status = "Netscape Navigator required.";
    alert("Netscape Navigator required.");
}
```

5. When you have made the necessary changes to the HTML document, save your new file with the name *js-five.html*.

```
〈HTML〉
〈HEAD〉
〈TITLE〉JavaScript Activity #5〈/TITLE〉
〈/HEAD〉
〈BODY〉
〈CENTER〉
〈H1〉
〈SCRIPT〉
    document.write("Hello World Wide Web!");
〈/SCRIPT〉
〈/H1〉
〈H3〉
〈SCRIPT〉
    document.write("Welcome to the exciting world of JavaScript.");
〈/SCRIPT〉
〈/H3〉
〈SCRIPT〉
    if (navigator.appName == "Netscape")
    {
        document.write("You are using Netscape Navigator.");
        window.status = "Netscape Navigator detected.";
        alert("Netscape Navigator detected.");
    }
    else
    {
        document.write("You are not using Netscape Navigator.〈BR〉");
        document.write("I'll bet you're using Internet Explorer.");
        window.status = "Netscape Navigator required.";
        alert("Netscape Navigator required.");
    }
〈/SCRIPT〉
〈/CENTER〉
〈/BODY〉
〈/HTML〉
```

Figure 4.11
JavaScript source code to set
the browser status line

Net Fun

Have you ever wondered what a professional language specification looks like? To be more specific, would you like to see the official language specification for JavaScript? If so, check out the following URL with your Web browser:

http://lom.pvrr.ru/java/jsspec/titlepg2.htm

This Web page contains a wealth of technical information about the JavaScript 1.1 scripting language. If some of this information seems to be a little over your head, don't worry! We will continue to lead you through the JavaScript learning process step by step. Just be glad that you are *using* the language rather than *defining* it!

6 Open your Web browser and view your *js-five.html* file. If you are running Netscape Navigator, your screen should look like Figure 4.12a. But if you are running Microsoft's Internet Explorer, your screen will look like Figure 4.12b.

Figure 4.12a
Your screen in Netscape Navigator

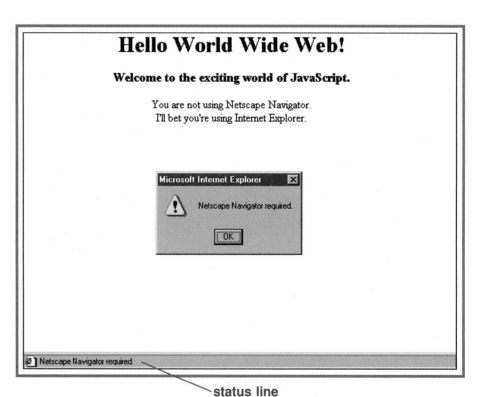

Figure 4.12b
Your screen in Internet Explorer

As we mentioned in Activity 4.4, the most common way for Java-Script to interact with a Web surfer is by means of the document.write() method. But the browser status line also can be an effective way of communicating information to the user. In this case, we simply have used the status line to echo the message displayed in the alert dialog box. However, it is much more common to see JavaScript programs use the status line to let the user know what it is doing. Whenever your script is about to initiate a potentially lengthy process (such as download a large graphic image, for example), it is a good idea to display an appropriate message in the status line. This can go a long way toward making sure that the user knows his system hasn't crashed.

THINKING ABOUT TECHNOLOGY

One way in which some JavaScript programmers utilize the browser status line is to display instructions to the user. In this case, it might make sense to display a message that tells the user what to do when the alert dialog appears. That is, the status line could include a message that tells the user to click on the OK button to continue processing the script. Why don't you go ahead and make this change? Try to make the message as informative as possible without using a lot of words. Can you do it? Yes, of course you can!

NET FACT

Hello, World!

The next time you are in your local bookstore, take a few minutes to skim through the first few chapters of several different programming books. In many cases, you will see that the first programming example introduced in these books demonstrates how to display the phrase "Hello, World!" in that particular language. Why do you suppose it is so common for authors to begin their books in this way? Well, the answer is simple.

In 1978, two employees of Bell Laboratories named Brian Kernighan and Dennis Ritchie published a book entitled *The C Programming Language.* This book has proven itself to be one of the most enduring programming tutorials in the history of computer software. Over the past twenty years, this book has undergone only one revision, and the second edition is still in print to this day! And as it turns out, the very first programming exercise in this book explains how to use the C function called *printf* to display the phrase "Hello, World." Though it is unlikely Kernighan and Ritchie intended to start an informal tradition among authors of programming books, that is exactly what they did! And although we took the liberty of modifying the phrase somewhat (to "Hello, World Wide Web!"), it is still based on this simple example from twenty years ago.

NET VOCABULARY

Define the following terms:

1. binary code
2. compiler
3. condition
4. interpretation
5. keywords
6. methods
7. objects
8. operators
9. parameter list
10. programming language
11. scripting language
12. ⟨SCRIPT⟩ and ⟨/SCRIPT⟩ tags
13. status line
14. syntax
15. token
16. Web browser

NET REVIEW

Give a short answer to the following questions:

1. How does JavaScript enhance the capabilities of HTML?

_____

_____

_____

_____

_____

2. What is a JavaScript object? What are object methods and object properties?

_____

_____

_____

_____

3. What JavaScript method is most commonly used to generate output?

_____

_____

_____

_____

4.   *What is the syntax of a conditional statement in JavaScript?*

_____

_____

_____

_____

5.   *In what ways does the alert() method differ from the document.write() method?*

_____

_____

_____

_____

Net Fun

How would you like to explore a commercial Web site that makes good use of JavaScript technology? Anyone who watches cable TV should be familiar with the service called "The Prevue Channel," which gives you a continuous listing of the TV shows scheduled for your particular area. Go to *http://www. prevue.com* to see how JavaScript can be used to implement the same service over the Internet. This is some serious JavaScript code!

EMBEDDING HTML TAGS IN JAVASCRIPT OUTPUT

Great Applications, Inc. is looking for a skilled Internet programmer who has a good understanding of HTML programming with JavaScript. In order to test the knowledge of potential employees, Great Applications is giving each candidate a simple HTML/JavaScript test. The test contains the 19-line source code listing found in Activity 4.2, and each applicant is given a simple task to perform. The instructions for completing the task are as follows:

- Remove the 〈H1〉 and 〈/H1〉 tags from the HTML file, and re-insert them somewhere inside the first script section. After you have moved these two tags, the resulting HTML file must *not* cause the browser to generate an error message, but the Web page should look exactly the same on the screen as it did before.
- Do the same with the 〈H3〉 and 〈/H3〉 tags. Move them to a new location within the second script so that the Web page continues to display correctly.

Can you do it? We're sure you can if you review Activity 4.3 carefully.

NET PROJECT TEAMWORK

Changing a JavaScript Program's Browser Orientation

As a team of three or four, study the HTML/JavaScript file you created in Activity 4.5. Pretend that Great Applications, Inc. has just assigned your group the task of rewriting this program so that it is oriented toward Microsoft's Internet Explorer (IE) rather than toward Netscape's Navigator. This means that you will have to change the JavaScript conditional statement, as well as the wording of the text strings inside the *if* and the *else* statement blocks in your *js-four.html* file.

When you have completed your changes, view the new file with Netscape Navigator and with Microsoft's Internet Explorer to make sure that it operates correctly in both.

Hint: The appName property will contain the value "Microsoft Internet Explorer" when Internet Explorer is running.

WRITING ABOUT TECHNOLOGY

In the introduction to Activity 4.3, we mentioned that the conditional statement is one of JavaScript's most powerful features. This claim is merely an echo of a statement made more than twenty years ago by a great computer scientist by the name of Joseph Weizenbaum. In 1976, Mr. Weizenbaum published a book entitled *Computer Power and Human Reason,* in which he presented the idea that the real power of computer systems is their ability to make decisions. Think about this idea for a while, and then answer the following questions:

How useful would computers be if they could not make decisions?

_____

_____

_____

_____

Describe the general structure of the JavaScript decision-making statement:

_____

_____

_____

_____

What does it mean to "evaluate a condition"?

_____

_____

_____

_____

Why do you suppose the *else* clause of the *if-else* statement is optional?

_____

_____

_____

_____

Client/Server Application Engineers

Wherever you may go throughout corporate America, you will find a high demand for software developers who can create fast, reliable client/server applications. The main idea behind a client/server application is that one process (or program, essentially) will run in a central location, and then multiple client processes, running in many different locations, will make requests of the server process and wait for responses.

Twenty years ago, this type of "distributed" application would be found only in large corporations, banks, or airline reservation agencies because they were difficult to install and expensive to maintain. However, now that the use of the Internet has proliferated throughout our society, the means to establish and utilize the client/server architecture is well within the reach of small businesses, government agencies, or even school districts. Unfortunately, though, having the means to create a client/server software system does not mean it is easy to find someone who can do it. That is why acquiring a solid knowledge of JavaScript technology could prove to be very profitable for you some day. JavaScript is frequently used on the client side of client/server applications, so you can be sure that there are a lot of companies out there just waiting to hire you. Don't miss this great opportunity!

Using Images with JavaScript

Chapter Objectives

In this chapter, you will use JavaScript to manipulate images. After reading Chapter 5, you will be able to

1 understand the names and usage of JavaScript events.

2 understand the purpose and syntax of JavaScript functions.

3 learn to create an image rollover.

4 learn to create a hyperlink rollover.

5 learn to create a cycling banner.

6 learn to display random images.

7 learn to create a JavaScript slide show.

JavaScript Terms

array

cycling banner (ad banner)

decrement

event

function

hyperlink rollover

image rollover

increment

index

instantiate

real number (floating-point number)

slide show

variable

Making Graphic Images Come Alive

In Chapter 3, we mentioned how important the effective use of graphic images can be to the overall success of a Web page. Well, that principle holds true whether the Web page is based on HTML or JavaScript technology. Standard HTML gives you the ability to do several interesting things with images, but JavaScript gives you some additional capabilities. In this chapter, we will focus on those features of JavaScript that are commonly used to make graphic images "come alive" on Web pages. Once you have learned these new techniques, you will quickly recognize their usage all over the World Wide Web. Then you will no longer need to wonder how the designers of these interesting pages were able to create such eye-catching effects.

Before you can accomplish anything spectacular with images, you will need to acquire an understanding of JavaScript events. For the purpose of this book, you can think of an **event** as a system-level response to the occurrence of some specific condition. Some of these conditions are generated by the Web browser software itself, but most of them are caused by the user performing some action. Such ac-

tions might include moving the mouse, clicking on a button object, or even selecting a block of text on the screen. But regardless of how a particular event is generated, JavaScript gives you the ability to create Web pages that react to it. And when these reactions are implemented skillfully, the user will definitely be impressed by your Web page.

Another important concept you will need to master when working with images is the notion of JavaScript functions. A **function** is nothing more that a segment of JavaScript code that can be invoked (or called) just like the document.write() and alert() methods you used in Chapter 4. In fact, there is really no difference between a method and a function except that methods have already been defined as part of the JavaScript programming environment. Functions, on the other hand, are written by you and may contain any number of JavaScript statements, including calls to JavaScript methods or other functions.

It may not be obvious to you at this point how JavaScript events and functions relate to the usage of graphic images in Web pages. But just be patient, and you will see the connection very soon. In fact, that is the very purpose of the activities in this chapter. We will be using events and functions with images to create some interesting effects that will improve the quality of your Web pages immensely. So if you are ready to get started, let's get to work! ∎

NET TIP
Using JavaScript Events

All of the activities in this chapter make use of one or more JavaScript events. However, there are several JavaScript events available that are not discussed in this chapter. But that doesn't mean you can't do a little "independent study" and learn how to use them on your own. Here is an alphabetical list of the JavaScript events that are available, along with a brief description of the condition that will trigger the event.

Event Name	Event Trigger
onAbort	The user aborted the loading of a Web page.
onBlur	The user deactivated an object (the object lost focus).
onChange	The user changed an object in some way.
onClick	The user clicked the mouse on an object.
onError	The JavaScript interpreter encountered a script error.
onFocus	The user activated an object (the object received focus).
onLoad	The Web browser finished loading a page.
onMouseOver	The mouse pointer passed over an object.
onMouseOut	The mouse pointer moved off of an object.
onSelect	The user selected (highlighted) the contents of an object.
onSubmit	The user submitted a HTML form.
onUnload	The Web browser unloaded a page from memory.

ACTIVITY

5.1

Objective:

In this activity, you will learn how to create an image rollover with JavaScript.

Teaching an Image to Roll Over

In Chapter 3, you learned how to include a graphic image in your Web page, and you also learned how to turn an image into a hyperlink. Now we are going to show you how to use the power of Java-Script to make a graphical hyperlink respond to mouse movement. To be more specific, we are going to show you how you can change the appearance of an image whenever the user moves the mouse pointer over it. This JavaScript programming technique is called an **image rollover.**

The first thing you need to know in order to implement a rollover is how to make use of the JavaScript events called *onMouseOver* and *onMouseOut.* The onMouseOver event is generated whenever the user moves the mouse over a particular object. Likewise, the onMouseOut event is generated when the user moves the mouse pointer off of the object. All you need to learn is how to use Java-Script to detect when these events occur, and then take some appropriate action. In this activity, we are going to display a blue arrow on the screen and then change that arrow to red when the mouse pointer rolls over it. We will then change the arrow color back to blue when the mouse pointer rolls off of the image. Sound simple enough? Then let's get to it.

1. You will need to use some graphics in this activity, which you will download from the *HTML & JavaScript: Programming Concepts* Web page. So, open your Web browser and enter the URL *www.swep.com.*

2. Click on *Computer Education* at the bottom of the screen.

3. Select *Products & Resources* on the left side of the next screen.

4. Select *Internet* from the Computer Education Categories box, and click *Go!*

5. Scroll down and look for the *HTML & JavaScript: Programming Concepts* Web page.

6. Click the Student Activities link, followed by the Activity 5.1 link.

7. Download the *bluearrow.gif* and *redarrow.gif* files to the exact same folder where you have been saving your Web pages.

8. Open your text editor or word processor, and type the HTML/JavaScript code exactly as it appears in Figure 5.1.

9. Save this file in the appropriate folder as *js-six.html.*

10. Open your Web browser if it is not already open.

11. View your *js-six.html* page. Your Web page should initially look like Figure 5.2a. But when you move the mouse pointer over the arrow image, its appearance should change to look like Figure 5.2b.

HOT TIP

Shortcut Address

A shortcut has been provided to the HTML & JavaScript: Programming Concepts *student activities home page:* htmljava.swep.com.

```
〈HTML〉
〈HEAD〉
〈TITLE〉JavaScript Activity #6〈/TITLE〉
〈SCRIPT〉
    blueArrow = new Image;
    blueArrow.src = "bluearrow.gif";
    redArrow = new Image;
    redArrow.src = "redarrow.gif";
〈/SCRIPT〉
〈/HEAD〉
〈BODY〉
〈CENTER〉
〈A HREF="webpage.html"
  onMouseOver="document.arrow.src = redArrow.src;"
  onMouseOut="document.arrow.src = blueArrow.src;"〉
〈IMG SRC="bluearrow.gif"
    NAME="arrow"
    WIDTH=320
    HEIGHT=200〉
〈/A〉
〈/CENTER〉
〈/BODY〉
〈/HTML〉
```

Figure 5.1
JavaScript code to create an image rollover

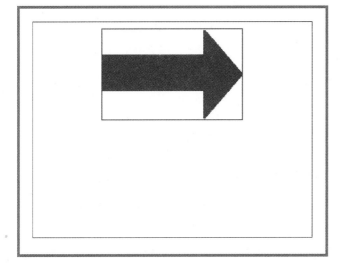

Figure 5.2a
Your Web page as it appears initially

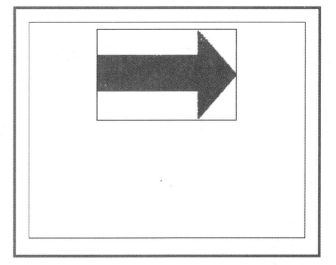

Figure 5.2b
Your Web page when the mouse pointer rolls over the image

Even though the HTML/JavaScript source code in Figure 5.1 is not very large, it does introduce several new features that you have not seen before. Let's take a minute to make sure you understand all of these concepts, because you will be seeing them throughout this chapter.

First of all, you should be aware that the ⟨SCRIPT⟩ and ⟨/SCRIPT⟩ tags appear in the header section of the HTML document rather than in the body section. This means that the Web browser will process the JavaScript code *before* it begins to display the contents of the document on the screen. This is an important point for this particular document because we want the browser to load both the blue and the red arrow images into memory before it displays the body of the Web page. If we fail to do this, the browser would not know what images to load when the onMouseOver and onMouseOut events occur, and the result would be a JavaScript error message.

Next, it is important for you to understand what the JavaScript code (Lines 5 through 8 of Figure 5.1) actually does. The statement in Line 5 (blueArrow = new Image;) tells the JavaScript interpreter to create a new Image object, and then to save a reference to that object in a **variable** that we have called *blueArrow*. (Remember that a JavaScript variable is nothing more than a name that is assigned to a literal value or to an object. Once this assignment has been made, the name can be used throughout the HTML document to refer to that particular value or object.)

The following statement, on Line 6 (blueArrow.src = "bluearrow. gif";), tells JavaScript that the source (src) property of the blueArrow object will contain the graphic image stored in the file *bluearrow.gif*. This is the statement that actually causes the browser to load the blue arrow image into memory. Once this task is complete, the next two JavaScript statements perform essentially the same function as the first two statements.

The statement on Line 7 (redArrow = new Image;) causes the interpreter to create a new Image object and assign it the name redArrow. The statement on Line 8 (redArrow.src = "redarrow.gif";) sets the src property of the object to the image contained in the file *redarrow.gif,* so the browser will load this image into memory also. Any questions about this part of your Web page?

The next concept we need to discuss here is the JavaScript event handling logic. This is an important feature of JavaScript because it demonstrates another way in which JavaScript code can interact with standard HTML tags. Until now, all of the JavaScript statements you have used were located between the ⟨SCRIPT⟩ and ⟨/SCRIPT⟩ tags, right? But JavaScript event handling statements are actually placed *within* a standard HTML tag. In this case, the statements that handle the onMouseOver and onMouseOut events are located within the anchor (⟨A⟩⟨/A⟩) tags. When the onMouseOver event occurs, the source (src) property of the arrow object contained within the document object is set to the src property of the redArrow object. Likewise, when the onMouseOut event occurs, the src property of the document's arrow object is assigned the value of the blueArrow.src property. Thus, when the mouse pointer rolls over the arrow image, the onMouseOver event fires (occurs), and the image source is assigned the contents of the *redarrow.gif* file. In a similar fashion, moving the mouse pointer off of the arrow image causes the onMouseOut event to fire, and the image source is assigned the contents of the *bluearrow.gif* file. Is this making sense to you? Good!

The final point we would like to address concerns the origin of the document.arrow object. How does the browser know what object we are referring to when we use the name arrow? The answer, fortunately, is very simple. If you look closely at the ⟨IMG⟩ tag we used to define the original anchor image, you will see that we included a new attribute that you have not used before. This attribute is called NAME, and its purpose is to allow you to assign a variable name to the image object. In this example, we gave the image object the name arrow, and since this image is part of our HTML document, it can be referenced in JavaScript code as document.arrow. This is getting fun now, isn't it?

Thinking About Technology

You may have noticed that if you click the mouse button when your mouse pointer is over the arrow image, your Web browser displays an error message. Why do you suppose this happens? Well, if you think about it for a minute, you should realize that the arrow image was defined as a hyperlink in this document, and the purpose of a hyperlink is to tell the browser to load a new HTML document when the user clicks on it. So look carefully at the *HREF* attribute of your ⟨A⟩ tag. What Web page file will the browser try to load if you click on this particular hyperlink? Obviously, the answer is the *webpage.html* file, since that is the file name assigned to the *HREF* attribute. But does this file really exist? Of course not. Someone will need to create it, right? We think that someone should be *you*! Go ahead and create a very simple HTML page, and then save it with the name *webpage.html.* Then view your *js-six.html* page again, and verify that your browser will really display your new page when you click on the arrow image. Don't forget that this new file must be saved in the same folder as the *js-six.html* file.

Net Fun

When you can spare the time, try spending an hour or two searching the Web for sites that include interesting image or hyperlink rollover effects. After you have made a list of the sites you like best, try implementing the same types of rollovers yourself. Even though some Web sites implement their rollover effects with Java, there is no reason why you can't imitate their ideas and create your own rollovers with JavaScript. If you can attain a thorough understanding of the concepts presented in Activities 5.1 and 5.2, you can create any number of eye-catching effects to enhance the appearance of your Web pages.

ACTIVITY
5.2

Objective:

In this activity, you will learn how to create a hyperlink rollover with JavaScript.

Teaching a Hyperlink to Roll Over

Now that you know how to make an image rollover, let's show you how to create a **hyperlink rollover.** As you might expect, a hyperlink rollover is very similar to an image rollover. The only difference is that a hyperlink rollover is triggered when the user moves the mouse over a hyperlink, rather than when the mouse rolls over an image. Makes sense, right?

So if you are expecting the JavaScript code required to make a hyperlink rollover to be similar to the code for an image rollover, you won't be disappointed. In fact, if we didn't tell you what changes to make, you would probably have to look at the new source code twice to determine what the differences are. Are you ready to give it a try? Then let's get to it.

1. Open your text editor or word processor and retrieve the *js-six.html* file you created in the previous activity.

2. Change the activity number to 7.

3. Next, you're going to make a few changes to the opening anchor tag, ⟨A⟩, that defines a hyperlink. Add the line, Next Page, as shown in bold here and in Figure 5.3.

   ⟨A HREF="webpage.html"
      onMouseOver="document.arrow.src = redArrow.src"
      onMouseOut="document.arrow.src = blueArrow.src"⟩
   Next Page

4. Then you will move the arrow image outside of the closing anchor tag, ⟨/A⟩, so that it is no longer part of the hyperlink reference. You will also want to add a paragraph tag, as shown in bold here and in Figure 5.3.

   Next Page
   ⟨/A⟩
   ⟨P⟩
   ⟨IMG SRC="bluearrow.gif"
        NAME="arrow"
        WIDTH=320
        HEIGHT=200⟩
   ⟨/CENTER⟩

5. When you're finished making these changes, your JavaScript source code should look just like Figure 5.3.

6. Save your new file as *js-seven.html.*

7. Open your Web browser and view your *js-seven.html* file. Your screen should initially look like Figure 5.4a. But when the mouse pointer rolls over the Next Page hyperlink, the arrow image will change from blue to red, as shown in Figure 5.4b.

```
⟨HTML⟩
⟨HEAD⟩
⟨TITLE⟩JavaScript Activity #7⟨/TITLE⟩
⟨SCRIPT⟩
     blueArrow = new Image;
     blueArrow.src = "bluearrow.gif";
     redArrow = new Image;
     redArrow.src = "redarrow.gif";
⟨/SCRIPT⟩
⟨/HEAD⟩
⟨BODY⟩
⟨CENTER⟩
⟨A HREF="webpage.html"
   onMouseOver="document.arrow.src = redArrow.src"
   onMouseOut="document.arrow.src = blueArrow.src"⟩
Next Page
⟨/A⟩
⟨P⟩
⟨IMG SRC="bluearrow.gif"
     NAME="arrow"
     WIDTH=320
     HEIGHT=200⟩
⟨/CENTER⟩
⟨/BODY⟩
⟨/HTML⟩
```

Figure 5.3
JavaScript code to create a
hyperlink rollover

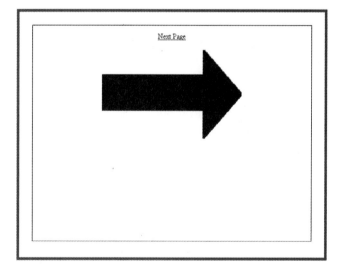

Figure 5.4a
Your Web page as it appears initially

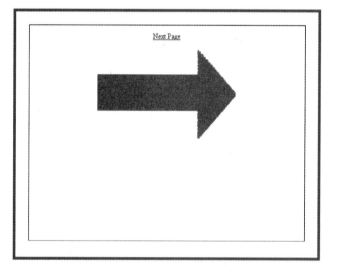

Figure 5.4b
Your Web page when the mouse pointer rolls over the
hyperlink

If you are an astute observer, you will notice that the JavaScript
statements in this HTML document (*js-seven.html*) are exactly the
same as in the previous document (*js-six.html*). So let's make sure
you have a solid understanding of what changes were made in the
HTML tags, and how those changes relate to the JavaScript code.

Chapter 5   Using Images with JavaScript

105

First of all, the ⟨A⟩ and the ⟨/A⟩ anchor tags no longer enclose the ⟨IMG⟩ tag, so the arrow image is no longer part of the hyperlink reference. Instead, the anchor tags now enclose the "Next Page" text you just added. This means that the onMouseOver and onMouseOut events will be fired when the mouse rolls over the new hypertext instead of when it rolls over the arrow image. However, the action performed by JavaScript code is the same as before, so the image changes color just like it did before.

You may be wondering why we inserted the paragraph tag between the hypertext and the arrow image. We did this because the paragraph tag forces the image down below the Next Page hyperlink. Otherwise, the image would appear to the right of the hypertext. (Feel free to remove the ⟨P⟩ tag and view the file again if you want to see what we mean.)

You may also be wondering why the arrow image was surrounded by a blue rectangle in the previous activity, but not in this one. The answer to this question is that in Activity 5.1, the image was defined as a hyperlink, and hyperlink images are normally displayed with a blue border by a Web browser. This is why the blue border is still visible when the arrow image is changed from blue to red. But in Activity 5.2, the image is *not* defined as a hyperlink, so the blue border is gone. Instead, the Next Page text is defined as the hyperlink, so it is displayed as blue and underlined, regardless of the color of the arrow image. Got it? (If you would like to know how to eliminate the blue rectangle in Activity 5.1, refer to *Net Tip: Know No Borders,* p. 107.)

THINKING ABOUT TECHNOLOGY

In Activity 5.1, we showed you how to create a rollover that reacts when the mouse pointer passes over an image. In Activity 5.2, we showed you how to create a rollover that reacts when the mouse pointer passes over a hyperlink. But now we want to know if you can create a rollover that will react to *either* condition? That is, can you make a small modification to your *js-seven.html* file that will cause the arrow image to change color when the mouse passes over the hyperlink *or* the image. Can you do it? Of course you can! All you need to do is move one HTML tag from its current position to a new position. Can you figure out what tag needs to move and to where? Try it!

Creating a Cycling Banner

Objective:
In this activity, you will use a JavaScript event and a JavaScript function to create a cycling banner.

When you are out "surfin' the Web," it is probably quite common for you to encounter commercial Web sites containing advertisements that are constantly changing. As it turns out, these **cycling banners** (also known as **ad banners**) can be created in various ways using different Internet technologies. However, one of the easiest and most efficient ways to create these types of advertisements is by using JavaScript events and functions.

A cycling banner is really nothing more than a sequence of graphic images that are displayed one after another with a small pause between each image. After all of the images in the sequence have been displayed, then the browser will cycle back to the first image and start the sequence all over again. This is the reason why this particular Web page enhancement is called a "cycling" banner.

You may think that creating a cycling banner takes a lot of time and effort, but this is not the case with JavaScript! In this activity, we will show you that it takes only a few minutes to integrate an effective ad display into your Web page. By utilizing a single JavaScript event, and by defining one simple JavaScript function, you will be well on your way to fame and fortune in the world of cycling banner design. Are you ready for this? Let's go for it!

1. Just as you did in Activity 5.1, you will need to use some graphics in this activity. So, open your Web browser and go to the *HTML & JavaScript: Programming Concepts* Web page.

2. Click on the Student Activities link, followed by the Activity 5.3 link.

3. Download the *lions.gif, tigers.gif, bears.gif,* and *ohmy.gif* files to the exact same folder where you have been saving your Web pages. (If you accidentally download the files to a different folder, your Web page will not function correctly.)

4. Open your text editor or word processor, and type the HTML/JavaScript code exactly as it appears in Figure 5.5.

HOT TIP
Shortcut Address

A shortcut has been provided to the HTML & JavaScript: Programming Concepts *student activities home page:* htmljava.swep.com.

NET TIP
Know No Borders

Whenever a graphic image is defined as a hyperlink in an HTML document, the Web browser will display that image with a rectangular border around it. But there are times when this border detracts from the overall appearance of the Web page. Fortunately, HTML provides Web page designers with the ability to adjust the size of a the hyperlink border with the BORDER attribute. By including a BORDER= statement in the ⟨IMG⟩ (image) tag, the content developer can make the hyperlink thicker or thinner or can make it disappear all together. To see how this attribute affects hyperlink images, try adding a BORDER=0 statement to the ⟨IMG⟩ tag in Activity 5.1. If you do this correctly, the blue hyperlink border should disappear. However, the image rollover should still function as it did before.

```
⟨HTML⟩
⟨HEAD⟩
⟨TITLE⟩JavaScript Activity #8⟨/TITLE⟩
⟨SCRIPT⟩
    imgArray = new Array(4);
    imgArray[0] = new Image;
    imgArray[0].src = "lions.gif";
    imgArray[1] = new Image;
    imgArray[1].src = "tigers.gif";
    imgArray[2] = new Image
    imgArray[2].src = "bears.gif";
    imgArray[3] = new Image;
    imgArray[3].src = "ohmy.gif";
    index = 0;

    function cycle()
    {
        document.banner.src = imgArray[index].src;
        index++;
        if (index == 4)
        {
            index = 0;
        }
        setTimeout("cycle()", 2000);
        return;
    }
⟨/SCRIPT⟩
⟨/HEAD⟩
⟨BODY onLoad="cycle();"⟩
⟨CENTER⟩
⟨IMG SRC="lions.gif"
    NAME="banner"
    WIDTH=400
    HEIGHT=100⟩
⟨/CENTER⟩
⟨/BODY⟩
⟨/HTML⟩
```

Figure 5.5
JavaScript code to create a
cycling banner

5 Save this file in the appropriate folder as *js-eight.html.*

6 Open your Web browser if it is not already open.

7 View your *js-eight.html* page. Your Web page should initially look like
Figure 5.6a. But after a two-second delay, the image should change to
look like Figure 5.6b. After an additional two-second delay, it should
change to look like Figure 5.6c, and then finally to Figure 5.6d.

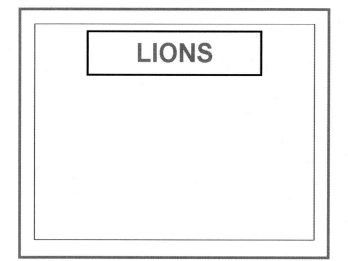

Figure 5.6a
The first image of your cycling banner

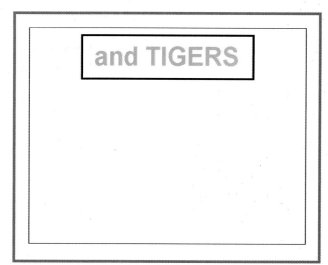

Figure 5.6b
The second image of your cycling banner

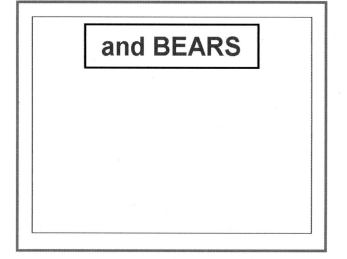

Figure 5.6c
The third image of your cycling banner

Figure 5.6d
The fourth image of your cycling banner

Once again, we introduced several important JavaScript concepts within a relatively small amount of source code. Let's go through the source code listing in Figure 5.5 carefully to make sure you understand exactly what's happening here.

First, take a look at Line 5 (imgArray = new Array(4);). Here we are creating a new JavaScript object, that you have not used before, called an **array.** An array is simply a collection of similar objects that can be accessed by means of a variable name and an index. Arrays are available in virtually every modern computer language, so it's important for you to become familiar with them. In this case, our array is defined to contain a maximum of four elements, and its variable name is called *imgArray.* In this case, the array will contain four Image objects, but arrays can contain any other type of JavaScript object as well.

Second, consider the JavaScript statements in Lines 6 through 13. These statements should look somewhat familiar to you, since they are essentially the same as those in Lines 5 through 8 of the previous activity. Line 6 creates a new Image object and assigns it the name imgArray with an index of 0. Line 7 then sets the source (src) property of this new object to contain the contents of the file called *lions.gif*. Similarly, the JavaScript statements in Lines 8, 10, and 12 also create new objects of type Image, and these new objects are assigned the name imgArray, with index values of 1, 2, and 3, respectively. The statements in Lines 9, 11, and 13 set the src property of these three new objects to the contents of files *tigers.gif, bears.gif,* and *ohmy.gif,* respectively. Now these four graphic images can be displayed very quickly by other JavaScript statements, which we will describe shortly.

Third, the statement in Line 14 (index = 0;) simply creates a JavaScript variable named **index** and assigns the value 0 to it. This variable will be used to access the various elements in the imgArray array.

Fourth, the JavaScript statements in Lines 16 through 26 define a function called cycle(), and this function will cause the images in the cycling banner to appear one after the other. This is accomplished by setting the src property of the document.banner object to the src property of the current element of the imgArray array. Then we increment the value stored in the index variable (using the ++ operator) in order to access the next element of our image array. The term **increment** means adding 1 to a value. Since the only valid indices for this array are 0 to 3, we must test the value of index to see if it has exceeded the acceptable range. In other words, if index contains the value 4, we must set it back to 0 in order to make the banner images cycle back to the beginning of the sequence. Then our final task is to set a timer that will call the cycle() function again after 2000 milliseconds have elapsed. (2000 milliseconds is equal to 2 seconds.) Are you still with us so far?

NET FACT

Zero-Based Arrays

Nearly every programming language supports the concept of arrays, but they don't all implement array indexing in the same way. If you define a 10-element array in Basic, Fortran, or Pascal for example, you would use index values of 1, 2, 3, . . . 10 to access those 10 elements. But some other languages (including C++, Java, and JavaScript) do not use this one-based indexing technique. Instead, they implement a zero-based technique that makes the valid array indices for a 10-element array 0, 1, 2, . . . 9. At first you might think that the one-based approach makes more sense because it is easier for novice programmers to understand. However, if you were to look at the low-level machine code generated by different language compilers, you would see that the one-based approach is less efficient for the computer hardware to process. This is one reason why professional programmers tend to use zero-based languages for their software development projects.

Finally, the last thing we need to explain is how the whole cycling banner process gets started. If you take a close look at the ⟨BODY⟩ tag of our HTML document (in Line 29 of the source code listing), you will see that we have inserted a new JavaScript event. This event is called onLoad, and it is triggered when the Web browser has finished loading the body of the HTML Web page. In this example, the browser loads the image called *lions.gif* (which is assigned the variable name banner by the NAME attribute), and then fires the onLoad event, which in turn causes the cycle() function to be invoked. The cycle() function will then be called continuously every two seconds in response to the JavaScript setTimeout() method, which is called inside this same function. Have you got it all straight now? We've learned a lot in this activity!

THINKING ABOUT TECHNOLOGY

A timeout value of 2000 milliseconds works well for this particular example, but sometimes different values can be more effective. Try changing the delay value in the setTimeout() method call to see what effect different numbers will have. And if you are extremely clever, you may recognize the fact that there may be occasions when providing a different delay value for each image in the banner sequence could be desirable. If you are feeling up to the challenge, try creating a second four-element array in the header section of your HTML document called delay. Then assign different values to each element in this new array (like 1000, 4000, 2000, and 3000), and use these values in the setTimeout() method call. That is, replace the constant value 2000 with the variable name delay[index]. If you can complete this task correctly, then you are well on your way to understanding the fundamentals of JavaScript arrays. You should be proud of yourself!

Net Fun

If you would like to see a good example of a commercial Web site that includes ad banners in its layout, check out *http://www.lantimes.com*. This is the official Web site of *LANTimes Magazine*. The ad banners run at the top of the screen, and if you watch them for several minutes, you should notice a pattern. The ad for a particular product will run through its images, and then those images will repeat. This repetitive process will continue for a certain length of time, and then an entirely new set of images will appear that advertise a different product. Why do you suppose the LANTimes Web staff has designed their ad banners to work like this?

ACTIVITY

5.4

Objective:

In this activity, you will learn how to display images in a random order.

Displaying Random Images

In the previous activity, you learned how to display a sequence of graphic images in a specific order. But there are also times when Web page designers want their images to appear in a random order. This approach is normally used when a particular Web site contains a large collection of graphic images, and the site owner would like the system to randomly select an image for display.

At first, you might assume that displaying images in a fixed sequence is much easier than displaying them in a random order. But this is not the case when you are programming in JavaScript. In fact, it actually requires fewer lines of code to display random images than it does to create a cycling banner. This is primarily due to JavaScript's built-in support for random number generation.

Since much of the source code for this activity is the same as for the previous activity, you will be able to use your previous file and make just a few changes. In fact, all you will need to do is replace the cycle() function with a similar function called select(). You don't even need to worry about downloading graphics files to the correct folder because we will use the same images as in the previous activity. Are you ready for this?

1 Open your text editor or word processor and retrieve the *js-eight.html* file you created in the previous activity.

2 Change the activity number to 9.

3 Next, you're going to delete the cycle() function and replace it with a new function called select(), as shown in bold here and in Figure 5.7.

```
function select()
{
    index = Math.floor(Math.random( ) * 4);
    document.banner.src = imgArray[index].src;
    setTimeout("select( )", 2000);
    return;
}
```

4 Then you will have to change the ⟨BODY⟩ tag so that the onLoad event calls the new select() function instead of the old cycle() function, as shown in bold here and in Figure 5.7.

⟨BODY onLoad="**select();**"⟩

5 When you are finished, the resulting file should look just like the source code listing seen in Figure 5.7.

6 Save your new file as *js-nine.html.*

7 Open your Web browser and view your *js-nine.html* file. Your screen should initially look like Figure 5.6a, 5.6b, 5.6c, or 5.6d, and then it should change every two seconds. Unlike the previous activity, the images will not appear in any predictable order.

```
⟨HTML⟩
⟨HEAD⟩
⟨TITLE⟩JavaScript Activity #9⟨/TITLE⟩
⟨SCRIPT⟩
    imgArray = new Array(4);
    imgArray[0] = new Image;
    imgArray[0].src = "lions.gif";
    imgArray[1] = new Image;
    imgArray[1].src = "tigers.gif";
    imgArray[2] = new Image
    imgArray[2].src = "bears.gif";
    imgArray[3] = new Image;
    imgArray[3].src = "ohmy.gif";
    index = 0;

    function select()
    {
        index = Math.floor(Math.random() * 4);
        document.banner.src = imgArray[index].src;
        setTimeout("select()", 2000);
        return;
    }
⟨/SCRIPT⟩
⟨/HEAD⟩
⟨BODY onLoad="select();"⟩
⟨CENTER⟩
⟨IMG SRC="lions.gif"
    NAME="banner"
    WIDTH=400
    HEIGHT=100⟩
⟨/CENTER⟩
⟨/BODY⟩
⟨/HTML⟩
```

Figure 5.7
JavaScript code to display random images

Let's quickly review the JavaScript concepts that are introduced in this activity.

First, we changed the function name from cycle() to select() because it more accurately reflects the purpose and behavior of the function. As a result of this name change, we also needed to modify the onLoad event statement in the HTML ⟨BODY⟩ tag so that it would invoke the proper function name. If we had failed to make this change, the Web browser would have responded with an unpleasant error message.

Second, we needed to include the appropriate JavaScript code to generate a random number, and then convert that number into a valid array index in the range 0 to 3. The JavaScript method random() (which is part of the Math object) is guaranteed to return a

real or **floating-point number** that is greater than or equal to 0.0 and less than 1.0. (A real number is a numerical value that includes a decimal portion.) Since numbers in this restricted range are not usable as array indices, we need to scale them to the proper range. In this case, we have four elements in our array, so we multiply (with the * operator) the random value by 4. Now we have a real number that is guaranteed to be greater than or equal to 0.0 and less than 4.0. The final step is to invoke the Math.floor() method, which will eliminate the decimal part of the resulting number. This means that the only possible values remaining are 0, 1, 2, and 3, and these are exactly the values we need to use as array indices.

Just to be sure you feel comfortable with this process, let's walk through an example. Let's suppose that the first three times the select() function is called, the Math.random() method generates random values of 0.137, 0.8312, and 0.54. When we multiply these numbers by 4, the resulting values are 0.548, 3.3248, and 2.16, respectively. Then when we run these new real numbers through the Math.floor() method, the final numbers stored in the index variable will be 0, 3, and 2, respectively. Obviously, these are all valid array index values, so the images displayed will be the contents of the files *lions.gif*, followed by *ohmy.gif*, and finally *bears.gif*. Or in other words, you would see Figure 5.4a, followed by Figure 5.4d, and finally Figure 5.4c on your screen. Do you understand?

Thinking about Technology

Let's suppose for a moment that instead of just four graphic images, your collection has increased to eight. What changes would you need to make to your JavaScript program to make it work properly with eight images? To start with, you would need to change your array size from 4 to 8, right? Then you would need to **instantiate** the four new array elements just like we did for the first four. Instantiation is simply the process of creating a new object and assigning it a value. What do you suppose would be the valid index values for the four new array elements? If you guessed 4, 5, 6, and 7, you are absolutely right! After you have completed this step, though, you still need to modify one more line of code. Can you recognize which one it is? If you read through this activity carefully, we're sure you can!

Creating a JavaScript "Slide Show"

ACTIVITY
5.5

Objective:
In this activity, you will learn how to use images and JavaScript to create an electronic slide show.

In the previous two activities, we showed you how to create JavaScript programs that will automatically change the image on the screen every two seconds. But sometimes it is more desirable to let the user decide for himself when he wants the image to change. When you allow the user to change the image by clicking on some object with the mouse, the end result is something akin to an electronic **slide show.** In this activity, you will create a JavaScript program that will provide the user with two hyperlinks labeled Back and Next. When the user clicks on one of these links, the image displayed will change appropriately.

In order to accomplish this task, you will need to modify the *js-nine.html* file you created in the previous activity. You will remove the select() function and insert two new functions named doBack() and doNext(). Then you will add some additional HTML tags to make the screen look good and to provide the user with the appropriate hyperlinks that will cause the slide show image to change. I'll bet you are excited to get started on this activity, so let's do it!

NOTE: For the sake of simplicity, we will be using the same graphic image files that we used in the previous two activities.

1 Open your text editor or word processor and retrieve the *js-nine.html* file you created in the previous activity.

2 Change the activity number to 10.

3 Delete the select() function and replace it with two new functions called doBack() and doNext(), as shown in bold here and in Figure 5.8.

```
function doBack()
{
    if (index > 0)
    {
        index--;
        document.slideshow.src = imgArray[index].src;
    }
    return;
}

function doNext()
{
    if (index < 3)
    {
        index++;
        document.slideshow.src = imgArray[index].src;
    }
    return;
}
```

4 Change the ⟨BODY⟩ tag to delete the select() function.

```
〈HTML〉
〈HEAD〉
〈TITLE〉JavaScript Activity #10〈/TITLE〉
〈SCRIPT〉
    imgArray = new Array(4);
    imgArray[0] = new Image;
    imgArray[0].src = "lions.gif";
    imgArray[1] = new Image;
    imgArray[1].src = "tigers.gif";
    imgArray[2] = new Image
    imgArray[2].src = "bears.gif";
    imgArray[3] = new Image;
    imgArray[3].src = "ohmy.gif";
    index = 0;

    function doBack()
    {
        if (index > 0)
        {
            index--;
            document.slideshow.src =
            imgArray[index].src;
        }
        return;
    }

    function doNext()
    {
        if (index < 3)
        {
            index++;
            document.slideshow.src =
            imgArray[index].src;
        }
        return;
    }
〈/SCRIPT〉
〈/HEAD〉
〈BODY〉
〈CENTER〉
〈H1〉My JavaScript Slide Show〈/H1〉
〈P〉
〈IMG SRC="lions.gif"
    NAME="slideshow"
    WIDTH=400
    HEIGHT=200〉
〈P〉
〈H3〉
〈A HREF=javascript:doBack()〉Back〈/A〉
     
〈A HREF=javascript:doNext()〉Next〈/A〉
〈/H3〉
〈/CENTER〉
〈/BODY〉
〈/HTML〉
```

Figure 5.8
JavaScript code to create a slide show

5 Between the center tags, you will need to add additional HTML tags and text to make your slide show look good on the screen, as shown in bold here and in Figure 5.8.

```
〈CENTER〉
〈H1〉My JavaScript Slide Show〈/H1〉
〈P〉
〈IMG SRC="lions.gif"
    NAME="slideshow"
    WIDTH=400
    HEIGHT=200〉
〈P〉
〈H3〉
〈A HREF=javascript:doBack()〉Back〈/A〉
     
〈A HREF=javascript:doNext()〉Next〈/A〉
〈/H3〉
〈/CENTER〉
```

6 When you are finished, the resulting file should look just like the source code listing shown in Figure 5.8.

7 Save your new file as *js-ten.html.*

8 Open your Web browser and view your *js-ten.html* file. Your screen should initially look like Figure 5.9a. But as you continually click the <u>Next</u> hyperlink, the image should change to look like Figures 5.9b, 5.9c, and 5.9d.

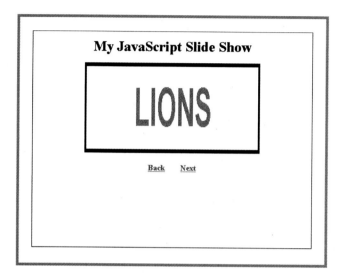

Figure 5.9a
The first image of your slide show

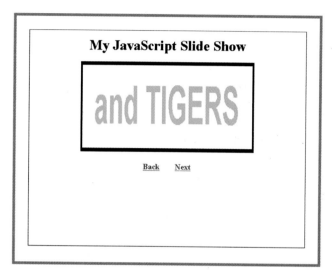

Figure 5.9b
The second image of your slide show

Figure 5.9c
The third image of your slide show

Figure 5.9d
The fourth image of your slide show

Once again we have introduced some new JavaScript concepts in this activity, so let's run through them to make sure nothing gets by you. The first several lines of JavaScript code (Lines 5 through 14) are the same as in the previous two activities, so you should feel comfortable with them by now. But you may not be completely familiar with everything in the doBack() and doNext() functions. Let's walk through them, shall we?

The first thing we do in the doBack() function is to test the value of the index variable. If it is greater than 0, then we know we are *not* displaying the first image in the slide show, so we need to back up to the previous image in the sequence. This is done by decrementing the value stored in index (with the -- operator) and then loading a new image source into the slideshow object of our HTML document. As you might expect, the term **decrement** means to subtract 1 from the current value of a variable. But you should note that if the current value of index *is* 0, then the doBack() function performs no action.

The contents of the doNext() function is, of course, very similar to that of the doBack() function. We first check the value of index to see if its current value is less than 3. If it is, then we know we are not displaying the last image in our slide show sequence, so we need to change the image on the screen. This is done by incrementing the index variable, and then setting the src property of the slideshow object to the next image in the list. But if the value of index is 3, then the doNext() function performs no action.

If you have a firm understanding of the material in Chapters 1 to 3, then you should feel perfectly comfortable with most of the HTML code contained within the body tags of this Web page. However, there are a couple of things that you have not seen before, so let's explain them also.

Net Ethics   Copyright Infringement

We mentioned in Chapter 3 that it is very unethical for Web page developers to download copyrighted images from commercial Web sites and then use those images for their own purposes. This obviously holds true whether the images are used in standard HTML pages or in JavaScript pages. But when you start developing JavaScript enhanced Web pages, you should also be aware that script piracy is just as unethical as picture piracy. In fact, it is not just unethical, it is also illegal! Although downloading and studying scripts that were created by other people is sometimes a great way to learn JavaScript, you must keep in mind that the copyright laws still apply. You should feel free to use publicly accessible JavaScript code for educational purposes, but you should not simply copy scripts from someone else's Web site to use on your own unless you get the owner's permission to do so.

You may have noticed that the HREF attribute of the <u>Back</u> hyperlink does not include a reference to another HTML document. Instead, it contains a reference to a JavaScript function named doBack(). Likewise, the HREF attribute of the <u>Next</u> hyperlink refers to the JavaScript function doNext(). This means that when the user clicks on one of these hyperlinks, the Web browser will perform the specified function rather than loading a new HTML page! Neat stuff, right?

The final item we would like to address in this activity concerns the three cryptic symbols   that occur on Line 48 of the source code listing in Figure 5.8. Suffice it to say that these symbols are HTML commands that tell the Web browser to put a little extra space between the <u>Back</u> hyperlink and the <u>Next</u> hyperlink. They are not required for this JavaScript program to function correctly, but they improve the appearance of the page somewhat. Feel free to remove this line from the file if you wish.

Thinking About Technology

Sometimes Web designers like to create slide shows that function in a "circular" fashion rather than in a "linear" way. This means that whenever the user reaches either end of the image sequence, the program will allow him to jump to the opposite end and continue viewing the images. In other words, if the user is currently viewing the first image in the slide show sequence and he clicks on the <u>Back</u> hyperlink, the next image displayed will be the last image in the set. Similarly, when the user is viewing the last image in the sequence and then clicks on the <u>Next</u> hyperlink, he will immediately see the first slide show image. Do you think you can modify your *js-ten.html* file to operate in this way? We're sure you can do it! If the answer isn't immediately obvious to you, go back and study the JavaScript cycle() function in Activity 5.3. It should tell you all you need to know!

NET VOCABULARY

Define the following terms:

1. array

2. cycling banner (ad banner)

3. decrement

4. event

5. function

6. hyperlink rollover

7. image rollover

8. increment

9. index

10. instantiate

11. real number (floating-point number)

12. slide show

13. variable

NET REVIEW

Give a short answer to the following questions:

1. What is a JavaScript event? How are events generated?

2. What is a JavaScript function? How does a function differ from a method?

3. How does an image rollover differ from a hyperlink rollover?

4. *What is a cycling banner? Why is it called "cycling"?*

_____

_____

_____

_____

5. *What is the purpose of the Math object methods random() and floor()?*

_____

_____

_____

_____

6. *What is a JavaScript slide show?*

_____

_____

_____

_____

PREPARING A REQUIREMENTS REPORT

Suppose that Great Applications, Inc. has just hired you to replace a JavaScript programmer who recently left the company. Your first assignment as a new employee is to prepare a report for your supervisor concerning one of the former employee's JavaScript programs. (The program in question is the cycling banner listing found in Figure 5.5.) He wants your report to contain a detailed description of what steps would be required to expand the content of the banner from four images to eight, and to make the delay value for each image variable. After reviewing the information presented in Activities 5.3 and 5.4, you should be able to create this report for your supervisor in practically no time. Isn't that right?

NET PROJECT TEAMWORK   Creating an Electronic Zoo with JavaScript

The management of Great Applications, Inc. has decided that they want to create an "Electronic Zoo," and they want to make it available to the public on their corporate Web site. Consequently, they have given your team the assignment of creating a JavaScript slide show that contains the images of many different kinds of animals. Each member of your team should spend some time searching the Web for suitable animal images, and then you must create a JavaScript slide show program to display them. Start with the source code listing in Figure 5.8, and then make the necessary modifications to get it to display the animal images you have collected. Some of the things you might want to change include:

- The Web page title
- The size of your image array
- The image file names
- The size (dimensions) of your slide show window
- The "last" index value in the doNext() function

WRITING ABOUT TECHNOLOGY

In Activity 5.3, we showed you how to create a cycling banner, or ad banner, as it is sometimes called. We also mentioned that there are numerous commercial Web sites that include ad banners, usually at the top of their Web pages. But one thing we haven't explained is the reason there are so many sites like this in cyberspace. It basically boils down to a monetary issue. The owner of the host site will charge other companies a certain amount to include their advertisements in the host Web pages. In this way, many Web sites can provide free services to their users, but still cover their own operating costs. Otherwise, many Web site hosts would go out of business in a very short time. So consider the following questions:

What types of businesses might choose to pay various Web sites to host their ad banners?

_____

_____

_____

_____

_____

What kinds of products and services are most likely to be advertised in this manner?

_____

_____

_____

_____

Why do you suppose most ad banners are defined as hyperlinks in the host HTML page?

_____

_____

_____

_____

What types of Web sites are most likely to host ad banners?

_____

_____

_____

_____

Web Advertisement Agent

There are many companies throughout the country who do so much business over the Internet that they need to employ a sizeable staff to make sure everything runs smoothly 24 hours a day. Some of these companies offer product advertisement services to other companies in order to help offset their operating expenses. And if these advertising services attract a sufficient number of customers, the host company will sometimes hire a Web advertisement agent to handle all of the various details associated with this part of the business. An ad agent is typically responsible for finding new customers, making sure their advertising needs are met, and then collecting the appropriate fees for providing this service. Some ad agents will even work directly with their customers to help them design ad banners that will be effective and catch the interest of potential customers. This type of job can sometimes get stressful, but it can also be very rewarding.

Creating Forms with JavaScript

Chapter Objectives

In this chapter, you will use JavaScript to enhance the functionality of HTML forms. After reading Chapter 6, you will be able to

1. understand the purpose and usage of JavaScript input controls.

2. understand the benefits of data validation.

3. learn to create an HTML form.

4. learn to enhance the functionality of HTML forms with JavaScript.

JavaScript Terms

array

buttons

checkboxes

controls/components

data validation

radio buttons

return a value

text fields

Making HTML Forms More Functional

In the last activity of Chapter 3, you received a brief introduction to HTML forms. In this chapter, we will begin by reviewing the information presented in Activity 3.5, and then we will show you how JavaScript can enhance the capabilities of HTML forms.

We begin the process of creating a fully-functional, robust form by defining the general layout of the form on a Web page. This step is accomplished by using the appropriate HTML tags, as described in Chapter 3. The next step is to identify the various objects in the HTML form with which the user will interact. Each of these interactive objects (also known as **controls** or **components**) must be given a name so that they can be referenced

within JavaScript code. Then the final step is to write the JavaScript functions that will be invoked when the user triggers a specific JavaScript event.

One of the most important concepts you will learn in this chapter is the idea of **data validation.** Data validation is simply the process of checking user input data to make sure that it is complete and accurate. Although it is not always possible to catch every error a user might make when filling out a form, there are many kinds of mistakes that can be detected. For example, if the user forgets to fill out a portion of a form, it is an easy task for JavaScript to detect the absence of required data and alert the user accordingly.

In order for you to learn these JavaScript form processing concepts effectively, we would like you to pretend that you work for a newly established pizza company called The JavaScript Pizza Parlor. As an employee of this new company, your job will be to create a Web page that will allow customers to place their pizza orders over the Internet. As you work through the following activities, you will learn how to make your electronic order form better and better.

We're sure you can't wait to get started, so here we go! ■

Net Fun

The pizza order form you have been working with in this chapter was obviously designed for educational, rather than business, purposes. Nevertheless, do you think there might be some pizza companies out there that really do sell pizza over the Web? The next time you get the chance, try doing an Internet search for pizza businesses that maintain their own Web page. How many of these businesses give you the ability to order pizza over the Web? You might be surprised at what you find!

ACTIVITY

6.1

Objective:

In this activity, you will create a simple HTML pizza order form.

Creating a Pizza Order Form

The first step in creating an effective order form for The JavaScript Pizza Parlor is to define its appearance on the Web page with the appropriate HTML tags. In this activity, you will use several tags and attributes that were introduced in Chapter 3 to make your form look appealing and well organized. The completed form will consist of nothing more than headings, labels, and user input controls, but it takes time and practice to make them all look good on the screen. Take note of the ways in which the heading, font, and break tags are used to control the final appearance of the pizza order form.

You should also pay close attention to the NAME attribute that appears in several of the following HTML tags. Although these names do not affect the appearance of the form at all, they are critical elements of the document. They will be used extensively by the JavaScript functions you will create in subsequent activities.

Let's get this show on the road, shall we?

1. Open your text editor or word processor, and type the HTML code exactly as it appears in Figure 6.1.

2. Save this file in the appropriate folder as *js-eleven.html*.

3. Open your Web browser if it is not already open.

CGI Script Developer

As you worked through the various activities in this chapter, you may have wondered how an actual pizza business would receive orders by means of a Web page. After all, the JavaScript code in these programs does nothing more than display various items of information on the screen. There are no instructions included in these examples that would actually cause the data entered into the form to be sent to another location, right? Well, you can rest assured that JavaScript *is* capable of sending information to another location, and this data transfer would normally travel through a Common Gateway Interface (CGI) that resides on a Web server somewhere. When the server receives the form data, it is processed by another program that would typically be written in CGI Script.

CGI Script looks a lot like JavaScript code, and it is processed in an interpretive fashion, just like JavaScript. CGI Script programs are capable of many different functions, but they are most frequently used to update a database system. This means that a pizza company, or any other type of business for that matter, could use any number of software packages to collect information from an electronic form that is distributed over the Web. But the main point we want to make here is this: CGI Script programs do not appear out of thin air. Someone has to write them, and that someone could be you! Anyone who can add a knowledge of CGI Scripting to their JavaScript coding skills should have a relatively easy time finding a job in the software field. Think about it!

```
〈HTML〉
〈HEAD〉
〈TITLE〉JavaScript Activity #11〈/TITLE〉
〈/HEAD〉
〈BODY〉
〈H1〉The JavaScript Pizza Parlor〈/H1〉
〈FORM NAME="pizzaForm"〉
〈BR〉
〈H4〉Step 1: Enter your name, address, and phone number:〈/H4〉
〈FONT FACE="COURIER"〉
Name:    〈INPUT TYPE="TEXT" SIZE=50 NAME="name"〉〈BR〉
Address: 〈INPUT TYPE="TEXT" SIZE=50 NAME="address"〉〈BR〉
City:    〈INPUT TYPE="TEXT" SIZE=16 NAME="city"〉
State: 〈INPUT TYPE="TEXT" SIZE=4 NAME="state"〉
Zip: 〈INPUT TYPE="TEXT" SIZE=8 NAME="zip"〉〈BR〉
Phone:   〈INPUT TYPE="TEXT" SIZE=50 NAME="phone"〉〈BR〉
〈/FONT〉
〈BR〉
〈BR〉
〈H4〉Step 2: Select the size of pizza you want:〈/H4〉
〈FONT FACE="COURIER"〉
〈INPUT TYPE="RADIO" NAME="size"〉Small
〈INPUT TYPE="RADIO" NAME="size"〉Medium
〈INPUT TYPE="RADIO" NAME="size"〉Large〈BR〉
〈/FONT〉
〈BR〉
〈BR〉
〈H4〉Step 3: Select the pizza toppings you want:〈/H4〉
〈FONT FACE="COURIER"〉
〈INPUT TYPE="CHECKBOX" NAME="topping"〉Pepperoni
〈INPUT TYPE="CHECKBOX" NAME="topping"〉Canadian Bacon
〈INPUT TYPE="CHECKBOX" NAME="topping"〉Sausage〈BR〉
〈INPUT TYPE="CHECKBOX" NAME="topping"〉Mushrooms
〈INPUT TYPE="CHECKBOX" NAME="topping"〉Pineapple
〈INPUT TYPE="CHECKBOX" NAME="topping"〉Black Olives〈BR〉
〈/FONT〉
〈BR〉
〈BR〉
〈INPUT TYPE="BUTTON" VALUE="Submit Order"〉
〈INPUT TYPE="BUTTON" VALUE="Clear Entries"〉
〈/FORM〉
〈/BODY〉
〈/HTML〉
```

Figure 6.1
HTML code to create a pizza
order form

4 View your *js-eleven.html* file. Your Web page should look like Figure 6.2.

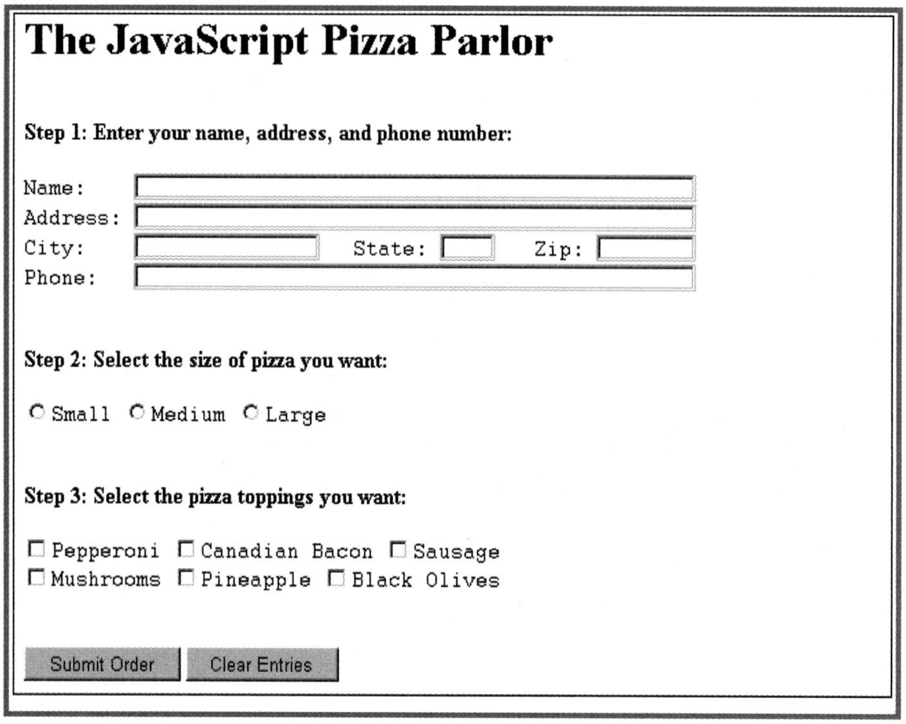

The JavaScript Pizza Parlor
Step 1: Enter your name, address, and phone number:
Name:
Address:
City:
State:
Zip:
Phone:
Step 2: Select the size of pizza you want:
Small
Medium
Large
Step 3: Select the pizza toppings you want:
Pepperoni
Canadian Bacon
Sausage
Mushrooms
Pineapple
Black Olives
Submit Order
Clear Entries

Figure 6.2
An HTML pizza order form

As we indicated before, all of the HTML tags used in this activity were previously introduced in Chapter 3. But to make sure you understand everything completely, let's review some of these concepts. Since the form itself is divided into three sections (or steps), let's take a closer look at each section to see exactly how it works.

The section we have called Step 1 consists of a heading and six labeled **text fields.** (A text field is an input control that allows the user to type a string value into a specific location on the Web page.) Each text field is assigned a size and a name, and   symbols are used to align the left edges of the Name, Address, City, and Phone fields.

The Step 2 section is composed of a heading and three labeled **radio buttons.** (A radio button is an input control that allows the user to select just one option from a set of options.) In this case, the radio buttons are labeled *Small, Medium,* and *Large* to correspond to the available pizza sizes. The Web browser will treat these three options as a set because they all have been given the same name (*size*).

The final section, called Step 3, consists of a heading and six labeled **checkboxes.** (A checkbox is an input control that allows the user to select any number of options from a set of options.) As was the case with Step 2, these checkboxes were given labels that correspond to the six kinds of pizza toppings available. The Web browser will also treat these six options as a set because they all have been assigned the name *topping.*

The final issue we would like to mention is that this pizza order form contains two **buttons** that are located at the bottom of the page. These input controls are defined with the ⟨INPUT⟩ tag just like the other controls, but the TYPE attribute is set to BUTTON rather than TEXT, RADIO, or CHECKBOX. If you try to click on either of these controls, you will find that they currently do not perform any action. Making these buttons functional is the object of the next two activities.

THINKING ABOUT TECHNOLOGY

If you want to be certain that you have a good understanding of HTML forms, try adding four new input controls to the pizza order form you just created. First, add a new text field labeled *Email:* that will be located directly below the *Phone:* field of Step 1. Next, add a new pizza size radio button, labeled *Jumbo,* to the right of the *Large* radio button under Step 2. And finally, add two new pizza topping options to the Step 3 section of the form. Label your two new toppings *Anchovies* and *Extra Cheese,* and position them to the right of the existing toppings (one per row). Can you do it? We knew you could!

NET FACT

The Origin of the Term "Radio Button"

The term *radio button* has been hanging around the software industry ever since Microsoft introduced its Windows operating system in the late 1980s. But there are very few people who know where the term originated or what it means exactly. Well, the answer is very simple. The Microsoft programmers who designed the Windows interface recognized the fact that it is often necessary to treat a set of options as mutually exclusive. In other words, only one option in the set can be selected at any given time. They also wanted to give this type of option a special name that would help the user understand its behavior. So, the term they chose to use was *radio button* because the behavior of these options is similar to the function selection buttons on old-style stereo systems. These old stereos typically contained several buttons labeled AM, FM, FM Stereo, Phono, Tape, and Aux that allowed the user to select a music source. And since it was only possible to listen to one music source at a time, pushing any one of these buttons caused any other selected button to "pop out." In addition, these mechanical radio buttons were usually round, so the Windows programmers gave this shape to their "radio buttons," too. Sometimes truth is stranger than fiction, right?

ACTIVITY

6.2

Objective:
In this activity, you will create a JavaScript function that is called when the *Submit Order* button is clicked.

Making the Submit Order Button Functional

Now that we have a solid HTML foundation for our pizza order form, let's start adding some extra functionality with JavaScript. The first thing we will do is add a JavaScript function that will be invoked (called) when the user clicks on the *Submit Order* button. In this case, we will simply display an alert box to let the user know that his pizza order has been submitted to The JavaScript Pizza Parlor. This is an important part of our form because it is usually a good idea to let the user know what the program is doing. (See *Netiquette: Give Me Your Feedback* on page 133 for more information on this topic.)

In order to get the *Submit Order* button to call a JavaScript function when it is clicked, you will need to make use of a new JavaScript event. As you might expect, this event is called *onClick,* and it is triggered whenever an input control of type BUTTON is clicked.

Now that you know what needs to be done, go ahead and do it!

1. Open your text editor or word processor and retrieve the *js-eleven.html* file you created in the previous activity.

2. Change the activity number to 12.

3. Next, you will need to add the *doSubmit()* JavaScript function definition, as shown in bold here and in Figure 6.3.

```
〈TITLE〉JavaScript Activity #12〈/TITLE〉
〈SCRIPT〉
   function doSubmit(pizzaForm)
   {
      alert("Your pizza order has been submitted!");
      return;
   }
〈/SCRIPT〉
```

4. The final change you need to make is to add the onClick event statement to the 〈INPUT〉 tag that defines the *Submit Order* button. This change is shown in bold here and in Figure 6.3.

```
〈INPUT TYPE="BUTTON" VALUE="Submit Order"
   onClick="doSubmit(pizzaForm);"〉
```

5. When you're finished making these changes, your new HTML/JavaScript source code should look just like Figure 6.3.

6. Save your new file as *js-twelve.html.*

```
〈HTML〉
〈HEAD〉
〈TITLE〉JavaScript Activity #12〈/TITLE〉
〈SCRIPT〉
   function doSubmit(pizzaForm)
   {
      alert("Your pizza order has been submitted!");
      return;
   }
〈/SCRIPT〉
〈/HEAD〉
〈BODY〉
〈H1〉The JavaScript Pizza Parlor〈/H1〉
〈FORM NAME="pizzaForm"〉
〈BR〉
〈H4〉Step 1: Enter your name, address, and phone number:〈/H4〉
〈FONT FACE="COURIER"〉
Name:    〈INPUT TYPE="TEXT" SIZE=50 NAME="name"〉〈BR〉
Address: 〈INPUT TYPE="TEXT" SIZE=50 NAME="address"〉〈BR〉
City:    〈INPUT TYPE="TEXT" SIZE=16 NAME="city"〉
State: 〈INPUT TYPE="TEXT" SIZE=4 NAME="state"〉
Zip: 〈INPUT TYPE="TEXT" SIZE=8 NAME="zip"〉〈BR〉
Phone:   〈INPUT TYPE="TEXT" SIZE=50 NAME="phone"〉〈BR〉
〈/FONT〉
〈BR〉
〈BR〉
〈H4〉Step 2: Select the size of pizza you want:〈/H4〉
〈FONT FACE="COURIER"〉
〈INPUT TYPE="RADIO" NAME="size"〉Small
〈INPUT TYPE="RADIO" NAME="size"〉Medium
〈INPUT TYPE="RADIO" NAME="size"〉Large〈BR〉
〈/FONT〉
〈BR〉
〈BR〉
〈H4〉Step 3: Select the pizza toppings you want:〈/H4〉
〈FONT FACE="COURIER"〉
〈INPUT TYPE="CHECKBOX" NAME="topping"〉Pepperoni
〈INPUT TYPE="CHECKBOX" NAME="topping"〉Canadian Bacon
〈INPUT TYPE="CHECKBOX" NAME="topping"〉Sausage〈BR〉
〈INPUT TYPE="CHECKBOX" NAME="topping"〉Mushrooms
〈INPUT TYPE="CHECKBOX" NAME="topping"〉Pineapple
〈INPUT TYPE="CHECKBOX" NAME="topping"〉Black Olives〈BR〉
〈/FONT〉
〈BR〉
〈BR〉
〈INPUT TYPE="BUTTON" VALUE="Submit Order" onClick="doSubmit(pizzaForm);"〉
〈INPUT TYPE="BUTTON" VALUE="Clear Entries"〉
〈/FORM〉
〈/BODY〉
〈/HTML〉
```

Figure 6.3
A pizza order form with a functional *Submit Order* button

7 Open your Web browser and view your *js-twelve.html* file. Your screen should initially look like Figure 6.2, but when you click on the *Submit Order* button, an alert box should be displayed, as shown in Figure 6.4.

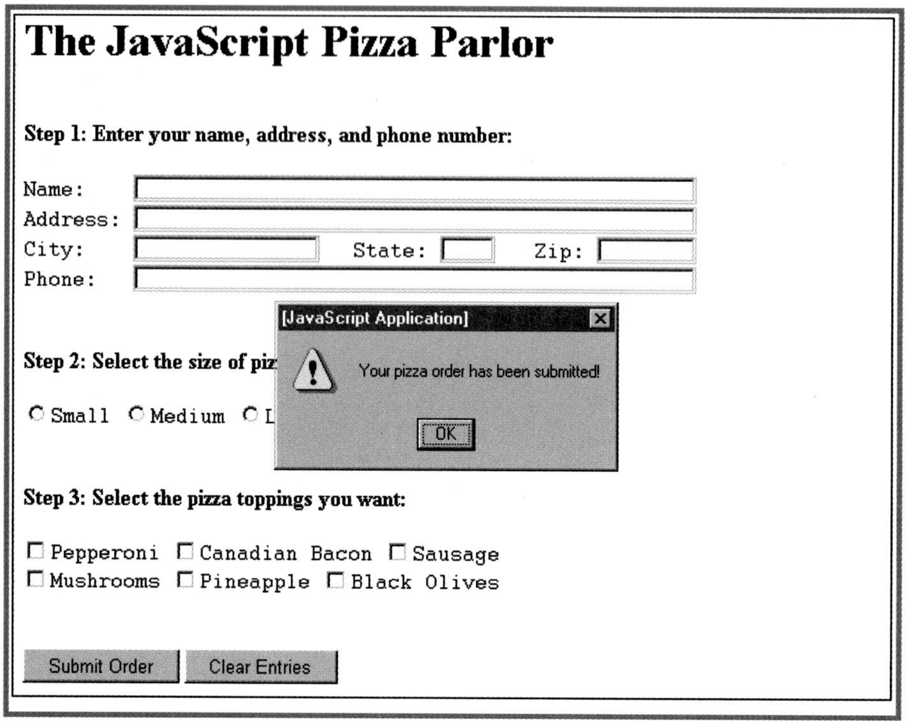

Figure 6.4
The pizza order form after the *Submit Order* button is clicked

If you think about this activity for a moment, you should recognize the fact that there is not much new here. The doSubmit() function you just added does nothing more than call the JavaScript *alert()* method, which was described in Chapter 4. And the concept of defining a JavaScript function was covered in some detail in Chapter 5. Consequently, you should feel very comfortable with this part of your program. As for the onClick event you added to the submit button ⟨INPUT⟩ tag, it also looks and acts just like the *onMouseOver, onMouseOut,* and *onLoad* events you used back in Chapter 5. In other words, you should have had no trouble at all understanding the concepts presented in this activity. Isn't that right?

NOTE: You may be wondering why the variable name *pizzaForm* appears in the doSubmit() function definition as well as in the onClick event string. We'll explain this in the next activity.

THINKING ABOUT TECHNOLOGY

As we mentioned in Chapter 4, it is sometimes useful to give the user more than one kind of feedback. Go back and review the information presented in Activity 4.5 about the browser status line. Then add a statement to the doSubmit() function that will cause an appropriate message to appear in the status line in addition to the alert box. This should be a relatively easy task to accomplish, don't you think?

Chapter 6 Creating Forms with JavaScript

Making the Clear Entries Button Functional

ACTIVITY 6.3

Objective:
In this activity, you will create a JavaScript function that is called when the *Clear Entries* button is clicked.

You probably know from personal experience that it is all too common for people to make so many mistakes while filling out a paper form that it is easier to start over than to correct the errors. Unfortunately, this is also true of electronic forms, especially when they require a large amount of information to be entered. For this reason, it is customary for Web page designers to include some type of "clear" button that allows the user to erase all of the form entries with a single click. In the case of our pizza order form, it would be nice to give the customer the ability to clear the form after an order has been submitted. Then a second order could be placed without having to change all of the existing data one entry at a time.

In order to accomplish this task, you will need to add another function to your HTML/JavaScript document called *doClear()*. Then you should add an onClick event to the ⟨INPUT⟩ tag of the *Clear Entries* button, just as you did for the *Submit Order* button in the previous activity. This event will call the doClear() function to erase any existing form data. Got it?

1 Open your text editor or word processor and retrieve the *js-twelve.html* file you created in the previous activity.

2 Change the activity number to 13.

Give Me Your Feedback

Over the past two decades, many software developers have learned the importance of giving users adequate feedback. In other words, it is essential for programs to give the user some kind of visual (or sometimes audio) clue as to what it is doing or what it has done. Think about it for a minute. What do you suppose an average computer user would do if he clicked the *Submit Order* button on an electronic form and nothing happened? Unless a message appeared to confirm that the order had actually been submitted, he would probably click the button again, right? Or maybe he might click it several more times in hopes that he might get some kind of response. Some other users might even erro- neously conclude that their computer has stopped responding and needed to be re- booted! This is an especially significant is- sue when a program has to perform an op- eration that takes a long time to complete. When your Web browser is downloading large graphic images over a slow Internet connection, for example, it is essential for it to give you some kind of visual feedback to let you know it is actually doing something. Otherwise, you would see a lot of impatient users rebooting their computers for no reason! So please be considerate of your users, and design your JavaScript programs to give lots of appropriate feedback.

3 Just above the closing script tag, add the JavaScript code for the doClear() function, as shown in bold here and in Figure 6.5.

```
function doClear(pizzaForm)
{
    pizzaForm.name.value = "";
    pizzaForm.address.value = "";
    pizzaForm.city.value = "";
    pizzaForm.state.value = "";
    pizzaForm.zip.value = "";
    pizzaForm.phone.value = "";
    pizzaForm.size[0].checked = false;
    pizzaForm.size[1].checked = false;
    pizzaForm.size[2].checked = false;
    pizzaForm.topping[0].checked = false;
    pizzaForm.topping[1].checked = false;
    pizzaForm.topping[2].checked = false;
    pizzaForm.topping[3].checked = false;
    pizzaForm.topping[4].checked = false;
    pizzaForm.topping[5].checked = false;
    return;
}
⟨/SCRIPT⟩
```

4 Next, you should add the onClick event to the ⟨INPUT⟩ tag of the *Clear Entries* button, as shown in bold here and in Figure 6.5.

```
⟨INPUT TYPE="BUTTON" VALUE="Clear Entries"
    onClick="doClear(pizzaForm);"⟩
```

5 When you have finished making these changes, your completed HTML/JavaScript source code should look just like Figure 6.5.

6 Save this file in the appropriate folder as *js-thirteen.html*.

7 Open your Web browser if it is not already open.

8 View your *js-thirteen.html* page. Your Web page should initially look like Figure 6.2.

9 Next, type some information into the text fields of Step 1, select a pizza size in Step 2, and select several toppings in Step 3.

10 Now click on the *Clear Entries* button at the bottom of the form. The entire form should instantly become blank and look like Figure 6.2 again.

As you can see, the steps required to make the *Clear Entries* button functional are very similar to those we used to make the *Submit Order* button active. However, there are some new concepts introduced in the doClear() function that are important for you to understand. So let's take a closer look at what these JavaScript statements are doing.

```
〈HTML〉
〈HEAD〉
〈TITLE〉JavaScript Activity #13〈/TITLE〉
〈SCRIPT〉
  function doSubmit(pizzaForm)
  {
  alert("Your pizza order has been submitted!");
  return;
  }

    function doClear(pizzaForm)
    {
    pizzaForm.name.value = "";
    pizzaForm.address.value = "";
    pizzaForm.city.value = "";
    pizzaForm.state.value = "";
    pizzaForm.zip.value = "";
    pizzaForm.phone.value = "";
    pizzaForm.size[0].checked = false;
    pizzaForm.size[1].checked = false;
    pizzaForm.size[2].checked = false;
    pizzaForm.topping[0].checked = false;
    pizzaForm.topping[1].checked = false;
    pizzaForm.topping[2].checked = false;
    pizzaForm.topping[3].checked = false;
    pizzaForm.topping[4].checked = false;
    pizzaForm.topping[5].checked = false;
    return;
    }
〈/SCRIPT〉
〈/HEAD〉
〈BODY〉
〈H1〉The JavaScript Pizza Parlor〈/H1〉
〈FORM NAME="pizzaForm"〉
〈BR〉
〈H4〉Step 1: Enter your name, address, and phone
    number:〈/H4〉
〈FONT FACE="COURIER"〉
Name:    〈INPUT TYPE="TEXT"
    SIZE=50 NAME="name"〉〈BR〉
Address: 〈INPUT TYPE="TEXT" SIZE=50
    NAME="address"〉〈BR〉
```

```
City:    〈INPUT TYPE="TEXT"
    SIZE=16 NAME="city"〉
State: 〈INPUT TYPE="TEXT" SIZE=4 NAME="state"〉
Zip: 〈INPUT TYPE="TEXT" SIZE=8
    NAME="zip"〉〈BR〉
Phone:   〈INPUT TYPE="TEXT"
    SIZE=50 NAME="phone"〉〈BR〉
〈/FONT〉
〈BR〉
〈BR〉
〈H4〉Step 2: Select the size of pizza you want:〈/H4〉
〈FONT FACE="COURIER"〉
〈INPUT TYPE="RADIO" NAME="size"〉Small
〈INPUT TYPE="RADIO" NAME="size"〉Medium
〈INPUT TYPE="RADIO" NAME="size"〉Large〈BR〉
〈/FONT〉
〈BR〉
〈BR〉
〈H4〉Step 3: Select the pizza toppings you want:〈/H4〉
〈FONT FACE="COURIER"〉
〈INPUT TYPE="CHECKBOX"
    NAME="topping"〉Pepperoni
〈INPUT TYPE="CHECKBOX" NAME="topping"〉Ca-
    nadian Bacon
〈INPUT TYPE="CHECKBOX"
    NAME="topping"〉Sausage〈BR〉
〈INPUT TYPE="CHECKBOX"
    NAME="topping"〉Mushrooms
〈INPUT TYPE="CHECKBOX"
    NAME="topping"〉Pineapple
〈INPUT TYPE="CHECKBOX"
    NAME="topping"〉Black Olives〈BR〉
〈/FONT〉
〈BR〉
〈BR〉
〈INPUT TYPE="BUTTON" VALUE="Submit Order"
    onClick="doSubmit(pizzaForm);"〉
〈INPUT TYPE="BUTTON" VALUE="Clear Entries"
    onClick="doClear(pizzaForm);"〉
〈/FORM〉
〈/BODY〉
〈/HTML〉
```

Figure 6.5
A pizza order form with a functional *Clear Entries* button

The first statement of the doClear() function makes use of the *value* property of the TEXT input control object. In this particular case, the text control was assigned the name *name,* and it is an element within the FORM object that we named pizzaForm. Therefore, we can easily clear the text value stored in that field by assigning an empty string (" ") to the *pizzaForm.name.value* property.

The next five statements of the doClear() function perform essentially the same action except that they reference the text control objects named Address, City, State, Zip, and Phone. Since these five controls also belong to the FORM object, they too are referenced with a pizzaForm prefix. In addition, we clear these five controls by assigning an empty string to their value property, just like we did with the Name field.

Clearing the pizza size value in Step 2 is done in a similar fashion, but there is a new concept at work here. Since we gave all three RADIO input controls the same name (*size*), the JavaScript interpreter will treat them as an **array** of objects. This means that we must use an index value to indicate which radio button we wish to access. The index values are assigned to the array elements will always start at 0, and they will increase sequentially for each new element encountered. In this case, the radio buttons labeled *Small, Medium,* and *Large* will be assigned index values of 0, 1, and 2 respectively. Each of these objects contains a property called *checked* that indicates whether the option is selected or not. We can clear all of these options simply by setting their checked property to the logical value *false.*

The pizza topping options of Step 3 work just like pizza size options of Step 2. Since we have defined six of these CHECKBOX objects with the same name (*topping*), they are treated as a six-element array. Their index values are, of course, assigned as 0 through 5, and they are cleared when their checked property is set to false.

Net Fun

The next time you have a little spare time, try surfing the Web to see how many sites you can find that include some type of electronic form. Are electronic forms just a small part of Cyberspace, or do they show up almost everywhere? How many of these forms are designed for the sole purpose of collecting some kind of information? How many are designed to give customers the ability to order some kind of product over the Web? How many offer some kind of service? Do you think this kind of technology is a passing fad, or is it really here to stay?

As a final note, we will keep our promise to explain the appearance of the pizzaForm object name in the function definitions and onClick event strings. As described in the preceding paragraphs, the doClear() function makes several references to objects within the pizzaForm object, but this object is not defined until later in the HTML document. So in order to process this function correctly, the JavaScript interpreter must be told that the pizzaForm object will be passed to it as a parameter by the onClick event. (Please refer back to Chapter 4 if you have forgotten what function/method parameters are.) In other words, it is this function parameter that links the pizzaForm variable name in the doClear() function to the actual HTML form defined later. Got it?

THINKING ABOUT TECHNOLOGY

In this example, we chose to give each of the text fields a unique name, but the radio buttons all got the same name, as did the checkboxes. However, this approach is not mandatory. In fact, we could just as easily have given all of the text fields the same name, and then they also would be treated as an array of objects. To make sure you understand this concept fully, try changing the NAME attribute of each TEXT input control to *info*. Then change the appropriate statements in the doClear() function so that your pizza order form continues to operate correctly.

NET TIP

Assignment vs. Comparison

You may have noticed that many of the JavaScript statements in this chapter use a single equal sign (=), while others use two equal signs (==). The reason for this is that all programming languages must make a distinction between assigning a value to a variable and comparing the contents of a variable to some other value. In the case of C, C++, Java, and JavaScript, the assignment operation is accomplished with the "=" character, while the comparison operation is performed with two "==" characters. So what happens if you confuse these two operators? Well, the answer depends on the language you are using. For many years, the C and C++ languages have been criticized because they allow the programmer to easily confuse the assignment operator with the comparison operator. This type of mistake is usually difficult to find because the program will compile fine, but it will yield unexpected results. The Java language designers, however, took this common pitfall into account when they defined its syntax rules. As a result, you will see a compilation error if you attempt to use the wrong operator. Unfortunately, the architects of JavaScript did not follow the Java experts in this regard. Like C and C++, JavaScript will let you use the wrong operator without a single complaint. Unexpected or erratic program behavior is the only clue you will get when you make this kind of mistake, so please use extreme caution in this regard!

ACTIVITY

6.4

Objective:
In this activity, you will learn how to validate the contents of TEXT input controls.

Validating Text Fields

Practically every business that provides its customers with an electronic form has the need to validate the data those customers enter in some way. Consider The JavaScript Pizza Parlor for example. What good would it do a pizza business to receive an order form where the address field was left blank? How could they possibly deliver a pizza to an unknown address? Or even worse, what if an inconsiderate prankster decided to submit dozens of pizza orders that were left completely blank? This type of scenario is one that would cause the business more harm than good.

For the sake of this activity, let's assume that the owner of The JavaScript Pizza Parlor would like your JavaScript program to accept only orders that have valid data in the Name, Address, City, and Phone fields. If a customer attempts to submit an order with any one of these fields left blank, the program will display an appropriate error message.

This is one type of data validation we promised you would learn in this chapter. So, let's get busy coding.

1. Open your text editor or word processor and retrieve the *js-thirteen.html* file you created in the previous activity.

2. Change the activity number to 14.

3. Just after the opening script tag, add the *validateText()* JavaScript function, as shown in bold here and in Figure 6.6.

```
⟨SCRIPT⟩
  function validateText(pizzaForm)
  {
    if (pizzaForm.name.value == "")
    {
      return false;
    }
    if (pizzaForm.address.value == "")
    {
      return false;
    }
    if (pizzaForm.city.value == "")
    {
      return false;
    }
    if (pizzaForm.phone.value == "")
    {
      return false;
    }
    return true;
  }
```

```
〈HTML〉                                               〈/HEAD〉
〈HEAD〉                                               〈BODY〉
〈TITLE〉JavaScript Activity #14〈/TITLE〉              〈H1〉The JavaScript Pizza Parlor〈/H1〉
〈SCRIPT〉                                             〈FORM NAME="pizzaForm"〉
    function validateText(pizzaForm)                 〈BR〉
    {                                                〈H4〉Step 1: Enter your name, address, and phone
        if (pizzaForm.name.value == "")                     number:〈/H4〉
        {                                            〈FONT FACE="COURIER"〉
            return false;                            Name:    〈INPUT TYPE="TEXT"
        }                                                   SIZE=50 NAME="name"〉〈BR〉
        if (pizzaForm.address.value == "")           Address: 〈INPUT TYPE="TEXT" SIZE=50
        {                                                   NAME="address"〉〈BR〉
            return false;                            City:    〈INPUT TYPE="TEXT"
        }                                                   SIZE=16 NAME="city"〉
        if (pizzaForm.city.value == "")              State: 〈INPUT TYPE="TEXT" SIZE=4 NAME="state"〉
        {                                            Zip: 〈INPUT TYPE="TEXT" SIZE=8 NAME="zip"〉
            return false;                                   〈BR〉
        }                                            Phone:   〈INPUT TYPE="TEXT"
        if (pizzaForm.phone.value == "")                    SIZE=50 NAME="phone"〉〈BR〉
        {                                            〈/FONT〉
            return false;                            〈BR〉
        }                                            〈BR〉
        return true;                                 〈H4〉Step 2: Select the size of pizza you want:〈/H4〉
    }                                                〈FONT FACE="COURIER"〉
                                                     〈INPUT TYPE="RADIO" NAME="size"〉Small
    function doSubmit(pizzaForm)                     〈INPUT TYPE="RADIO" NAME="size"〉Medium
    {                                                〈INPUT TYPE="RADIO" NAME="size"〉Large〈BR〉
        if (validateText(pizzaForm) == false)        〈/FONT〉
        {                                            〈BR〉
          alert("Required data missing in Step 1");  〈BR〉
          return;                                    〈H4〉Step 3: Select the pizza toppings you want:〈/H4〉
        }                                            〈FONT FACE="COURIER"〉
    alert("Your pizza order has been submitted!");   〈INPUT TYPE="CHECKBOX"
    return;                                                 NAME="topping"〉Pepperoni
}                                                    〈INPUT TYPE="CHECKBOX" NAME="topping"〉Ca-
                                                     nadian Bacon
function doClear(pizzaForm)                          〈INPUT TYPE="CHECKBOX"
{                                                           NAME="topping"〉Sausage〈BR〉
    pizzaForm.name.value = "";                       〈INPUT TYPE="CHECKBOX"
    pizzaForm.address.value = "";                           NAME="topping"〉Mushrooms
    pizzaForm.city.value = "";                       〈INPUT TYPE="CHECKBOX"
    pizzaForm.state.value = "";                             NAME="topping"〉Pineapple
    pizzaForm.zip.value = "";                        〈INPUT TYPE="CHECKBOX"
    pizzaForm.phone.value = "";                             NAME="topping"〉Black Olives〈BR〉
    pizzaForm.size[0].checked = false;               〈/FONT〉
    pizzaForm.size[1].checked = false;               〈BR〉
    pizzaForm.size[2].checked = false;               〈BR〉
    pizzaForm.topping[0].checked = false;            〈INPUT TYPE="BUTTON" VALUE="Submit Order"
    pizzaForm.topping[1].checked = false;                   onClick="doSubmit(pizzaForm);"〉
    pizzaForm.topping[2].checked = false;            〈INPUT TYPE="BUTTON" VALUE="Clear Entries"
    pizzaForm.topping[3].checked = false;                   onClick="doClear(pizzaForm);"〉
    pizzaForm.topping[4].checked = false;            〈/FORM〉
    pizzaForm.topping[5].checked = false;            〈/BODY〉
    return;                                          〈/HTML〉
    }
〈/SCRIPT〉
```

Figure 6.6
A JavaScript form that validates
text fields

④ Finally, add an *if* statement to the doSubmit() function as shown in bold here and in Figure 6.6.

```
function doSubmit(pizzaForm)
{
    if (validateText(pizzaForm) == false)
    {
        alert("Required data missing in Step 1");
        return;
    }
```

⑤ When you are finished making these changes, the resulting file should look just like the source code listing seen in Figure 6.6.

⑥ Save your new file as *js-fourteen.html.*

⑦ Open your Web browser and view your *js-fourteen.html* file. If at any time you click on the *Submit Order* button when any one of the required text fields is blank, you will see the error message in Figure 6.7.

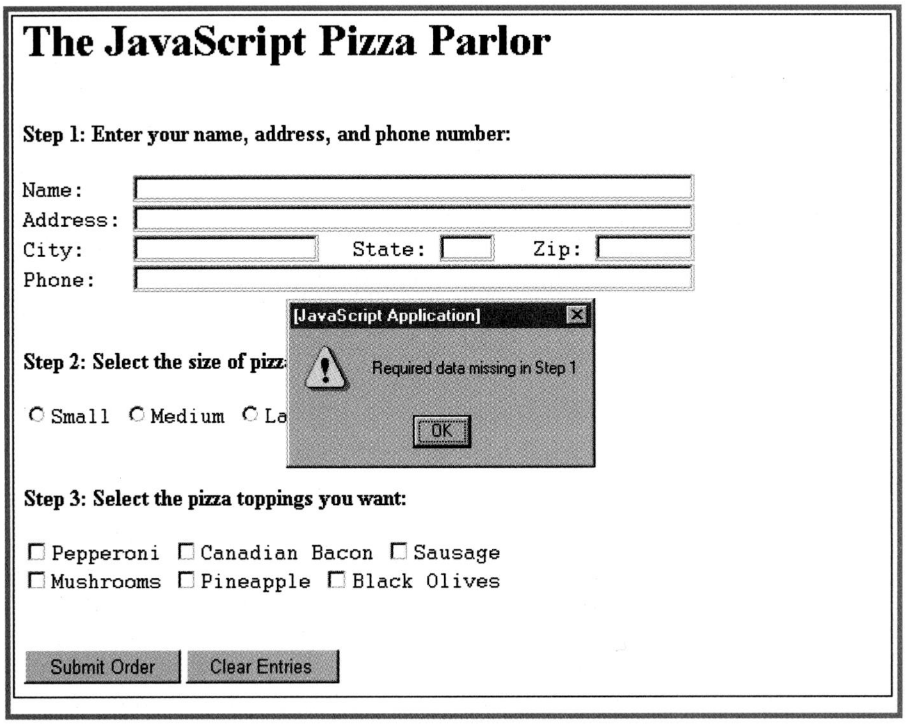

The JavaScript Pizza Parlor

Step 1: Enter your name, address, and phone number:

Name:
Address:
City: State: Zip:
Phone:

Step 2: Select the size of pizz

○ Small ○ Medium ○ La

[JavaScript Application] ⚠ Required data missing in Step 1 [OK]

Step 3: Select the pizza toppings you want:

☐ Pepperoni ☐ Canadian Bacon ☐ Sausage
☐ Mushrooms ☐ Pineapple ☐ Black Olives

[Submit Order] [Clear Entries]

Figure 6.7
A text field validation error message

As is often the case, we have added a relatively small amount of JavaScript code to our Web page, but this code illustrates a couple of important concepts.

First, the validateText() function is a little different from any other function you have written up to now because it **returns a value.** Returning a value means that whenever the function is called (in the doSubmit() function in this case), its name is essentially replaced by the value it returns. The validateText() function can only return one of two possible values: false or true. The false value is returned if the value property of the Name object, the Address object, the City object, or the Phone object is an empty string. That is, the false value is returned if any one of these fields is blank. But if none of the required text fields are blank, then the function returns a true value.

Second, the return value of the validateText() function is compared to the false value by the new "if statement" in the doSubmit() function. If the return value is false, then the doSubmit() function displays an alert box to let the user know he or she has left a required text field blank. Otherwise, the user will see a different alert box confirming that the pizza order has been submitted. Is this concept clear to you now? Good!

NOTE: If you are curious as to why the doClear() function uses a single equal sign (=) but the validateText() function uses two equal signs (==), please refer to *Net Tip: Assignment vs. Comparison*, found on page 137.

Thinking About Technology

Just to be sure that you understand the data validation technique at work here, let's see if you can add something new to your program. Pretend that the owner of The JavaScript Pizza Parlor wants to do a mass mailing of coupons to everyone who has ever ordered a pizza over the Web. In order to do this, he needs to make sure that customers enter valid data in the State and Zip text fields. Go ahead and add the appropriate code to the validateText() function so that it checks for empty strings in these two fields, also. This should be an easy task for you by now, right?

NET TIP

The Logical NOT Operator

Like C, C++, and Java, JavaScript gives you the ability to invert the value of a logical variable with the NOT operator (!). In other words, you can invert a true value to false or a false value to true by placing a single exclamation point in front of the variable. This operator is most commonly used when the programmer wants to test for a false condition. This means that wherever a variable (or function return value) is being compared to the false value (== false), the comparison can be shortened by using the ! operator instead. Here's a specific example:

if (validateText() == false) is equivalent to **if (!validateText())**

The preferred way of testing for a false value is a matter of personal taste. However, it is very common to see novice programmers use the former approach, while professional coders tend to use the latter technique. But either way will work just fine.

ACTIVITY
6.5

Objective:

In this activity, you will learn to validate radio button selections.

Validating Radio Buttons

Now that you know how to check for blank text fields, let's consider another type of data validation. In Step 2 of our pizza order form, we ask the customer to select the size of pizza they want. But what will happen if he fails to do this? As of now, the order will be submitted whether this information is available or not. This means that the person who receives the order at The JavaScript Pizza Parlor will have no idea what size of pizza the customer wants.

Fortunately, we will be adding some new JavaScript code in this activity that will prevent this situation from occurring. All we have to do is add another data validation function to our program and a new "if statement" to the existing doSubmit() function.

Are you ready to complete this final activity? Then let's go for it!

1. Open your text editor or word processor and retrieve the *js-fourteen.html* file you created in the previous activity.

2. Change the activity number to 15.

3. Next, insert a new function called *validateRadio()* to the ⟨SCRIPT⟩ section of your file, as shown in bold here and in Figure 6.8.

```
function validateRadio(pizzaForm)
{
    if (pizzaForm.size[0].checked == true)
    {
       return true;
    }
    if (pizzaForm.size[1].checked == true)
    {
       return true;
    }
    if (pizzaForm.size[2].checked == true)
    {
       return true;
    }
    return false;
}
```

4. Lastly, you should add a new "if statement" to the doSubmit() function as shown in bold here and in Figure 6.8.

```
if (validateRadio(pizzaForm) == false)
{
    alert("Required data missing in Step 2");
    return;
}
```

5. When you are finished, the resulting file should look just like the source code listing shown in Figure 6.8.

```
<HTML>
<HEAD>
<TITLE>JavaScript Activity #15</TITLE>
<SCRIPT>
    function validateText(pizzaForm)
    {
        if (pizzaForm.name.value == "")
        {
            return false;
        }
        if (pizzaForm.address.value == "")
        {
            return false;
        }
        if (pizzaForm.city.value == "")
        {
            return false;
        }
        if (pizzaForm.phone.value == "")
        {
            return false;
        }
        return true;
    }

    function validateRadio(pizzaForm)
    {
        if (pizzaForm.size[0].checked == true)
        {
            return true;
        }
        if (pizzaForm.size[1].checked == true)
        {
            return true;
        }
        if (pizzaForm.size[2].checked == true)
        {
            return true;
        }
        return false;
    }

    function doSubmit(pizzaForm)
    {
        if (validateText(pizzaForm) == false)
        {
            alert("Required data missing in Step 1");
            return;
        }
        if (validateRadio(pizzaForm) == false)
        {
            alert("Required data missing in Step 2");
            return;
        }
        alert("Your pizza order has been submitted!");
        return;
    }

    function doClear(pizzaForm)
    {
        pizzaForm.name.value = "";
        pizzaForm.address.value = "";
        pizzaForm.city.value = "";
        pizzaForm.state.value = "";
        pizzaForm.zip.value = "";
        pizzaForm.phone.value = "";
        pizzaForm.size[0].checked = false;
        pizzaForm.size[1].checked = false;
        pizzaForm.size[2].checked = false;
        pizzaForm.topping[0].checked = false;
        pizzaForm.topping[1].checked = false;
        pizzaForm.topping[2].checked = false;
        pizzaForm.topping[3].checked = false;
        pizzaForm.topping[4].checked = false;
        pizzaForm.topping[5].checked = false;
        return;
    }
</SCRIPT>
</HEAD>
<BODY>
<H1>The JavaScript Pizza Parlor</H1>
<FORM NAME="pizzaForm">
<BR>
<H4>Step 1: Enter your name, address, and phone num-
    ber:</H4>
<FONT FACE="COURIER">
Name:    <INPUT TYPE="TEXT"
    SIZE=50 NAME="name"><BR>
Address: <INPUT TYPE="TEXT" SIZE=50
    NAME="address"><BR>
City:    <INPUT TYPE="TEXT"
    SIZE=16 NAME="city">
State: <INPUT TYPE="TEXT" SIZE=4 NAME="state">
Zip: <INPUT TYPE="TEXT" SIZE=8 NAME="zip"><BR>
Phone:   <INPUT TYPE="TEXT" SIZE=50
    NAME="phone"><BR>
</FONT>
<BR>
<BR>
<H4>Step 2: Select the size of pizza you want:</H4>
<FONT FACE="COURIER">
<INPUT TYPE="RADIO" NAME="size">Small
<INPUT TYPE="RADIO" NAME="size">Medium
<INPUT TYPE="RADIO" NAME="size">Large<BR>
</FONT>
<BR>
<BR>
<H4>Step 3: Select the pizza toppings you want:</H4>
<FONT FACE="COURIER">
<INPUT TYPE="CHECKBOX" NAME="topping">Pepperoni
<INPUT TYPE="CHECKBOX" NAME="topping">Canadian
    Bacon
<INPUT TYPE="CHECKBOX" NAME="topping">Sausage
    <BR>
<INPUT TYPE="CHECKBOX" NAME="topping">
    Mushrooms
<INPUT TYPE="CHECKBOX" NAME="topping">Pineapple
<INPUT TYPE="CHECKBOX" NAME="topping">Black
    Olives<BR>
</FONT>
<BR>
<BR>
<INPUT TYPE="BUTTON" VALUE="Submit Order"
    onClick="doSubmit(pizzaForm);">
<INPUT TYPE="BUTTON" VALUE="Clear Entries"
    onClick="doClear(pizzaForm);">
</FORM>
</BODY>
</HTML>
```

Figure 6.8
A JavaScript form that validates radio
button selections

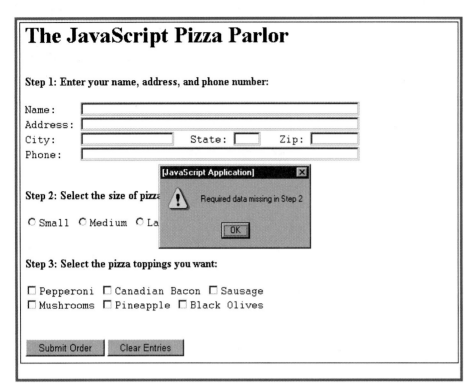

The JavaScript Pizza Parlor

Step 1: Enter your name, address, and phone number:

```
Name:    [                                      ]
Address: [                                      ]
City:    [                ] State: [  ] Zip: [      ]
Phone:   [                                      ]
```

[JavaScript Application]   [×]

⚠ Required data missing in Step 2

[OK]

Step 2: Select the size of pizza

○ Small ○ Medium ○ La

Step 3: Select the pizza toppings you want:

☐ Pepperoni ☐ Canadian Bacon ☐ Sausage
☐ Mushrooms ☐ Pineapple ☐ Black Olives

[Submit Order] [Clear Entries]

Figure 6.9
A radio button validation error
message

6 Save your new file as
js-fifteen.html.

7 Open your Web browser
and view your *js-fifteen.
html* file. Your Web page
should initially look like
Figure 6.2. But if you click
on the *Submit Order* button before the pizza size
has been selected, you will
see an alert box, as
shown in Figure 6.9.

The main idea behind
this activity is similar to the
previous activity, but let's
make sure you understand
the subtle differences.

In order to validate the
contents of a text field, we
check the contents of the object's value property to see if it contains
an empty string. But to validate a set of radio buttons, we need to
test the value of each object's checked property to see if it is set to
true or false. Consequently, the validateRadio() function sequentially
tests the value of each checked property in the object set, and returns a true value if it encounters a selected radio button. But if
none of the radio buttons in the set is selected, the function returns
a false value.

The true/false value returned by the validateRadio() function is evaluated by the doSubmit() function, just as it was for the validateText()
function. If the return value is false, then the user will see an appropriate alert box to let him know that Step 2 was not completed correctly. The end result of this activity is that customers will not be
able to submit an order to The JavaScript Pizza Parlor without selecting a pizza size first. Understand?

THINKING ABOUT TECHNOLOGY

Suppose that the owner of The JavaScript Pizza Parlor has decided that
the customer must select at least one pizza topping before the order
form can be considered valid. Can you write an additional function
(called *validateCheckbox()*) to validate Step 3 of the form? Can you also
add a new "if statement" to the doSubmit() function to test the return
value of your new function and display an alert box if the data validation
fails? Give it a try. We know you can do it!

NET VOCABULARY

Define the following terms:

1. array

2. buttons

3. checkboxes

4. controls/components

5. data validation

6. radio buttons

7. return a value

8. text fields

NET REVIEW

Give a short answer to the following questions:

1. What is an input control or component?

_____

_____

_____

_____

_____

2. How are text fields, radio buttons, checkboxes, and buttons defined in HTML?

_____

_____

_____

_____

_____

3. What is data validation? Why is it important?

_____

_____

_____

_____

_____

4. How do you validate the contents of a text field?

_____

_____

_____

_____

5. How do you validate a set of radio buttons?

_____

_____

_____

_____

ADDING A DROP-DOWN LIST TO A FORM

Suppose that Great Applications, Inc. has just won a major business contract with a pizza company called The Electronic Pizza Place. This company wants Great Applications to create a Web-based pizza order form like the one you created for The JavaScript Pizza Parlor in Activity 6.5. However, The Electronic Pizza Place only does business in the "four-corners" area of the United States, so they want the *state* text field replaced by a drop-down list that contains the two-letter abbreviations for Arizona (AZ), Colorado (CO), New Mexico (NM), and Utah (UT). Since you now have significant experience with this kind of project, Great Applications wants to hire you to create this electronic form. Can you do it?

Hint: If you don't remember how to create a drop-down list control, refer back to Activity 3.5 in Chapter 3.

NET PROJECT TEAMWORK   Improved User Feedback

Your supervisor at Great Applications, Inc. is fairly happy with the electronic order form your team has created for The JavaScript Pizza Parlor. However, he is not completely satisfied with the behavior of the form when one of the data validation functions fails. If a required text field in Step 1 is left blank, for example, he would like the error message that appears to specify which field is empty. In addition, he would like the cursor to appear in that particular text field when the user dismisses the alert box. And for one final change, he would also like the Step 2 error message reworded so that it includes the words "pizza size" in some way.

In order to accomplish this assignment, your team will need to remove the generic error message from the doSubmit() function and insert specific error messages into the validateText() function. Your team will also need to make use of the *focus()* method to get the cursor into the appropriate text field. Can your team get the job done?

Hint: To get the text cursor into the Name field, you could use the following JavaScript statement:

pizzaForm.name.focus();

WRITING ABOUT TECHNOLOGY

In this chapter, we have discussed the concept of data validation at length. In Activities 6.4 and 6.5, you have learned to implement two simple validation techniques. But if you were asked to explain the concept to a fellow student, including reasons why it is important, could you do it? Data validation is a fundamental part of virtually every professional computer program, no matter what type of program it is or in what language it was written. So, it essential that you attain a solid understanding of the concept. To help make sure you do, answer the following questions:

What types of data must be validated for a typical form?

_____

_____

_____

_____

Is checking for blank fields always sufficient for text validation? Explain.

_____

_____

_____

_____

What characteristics of a Zip Code field could be tested for validity?

_____

_____

_____

_____

Is it always possible for a computer program to validate every field on a form? Why or why not?

_____

_____

_____

_____

Ad banner
See Cycling Banner.

Angle brackets
HTML tags appear in pairs and are enclosed in angle brackets. The brackets can be found on the comma and period keys on the keyboard.

Array
A collection of similar objects that are accessed by a variable name and an index. When you give several controls the same name, they are considered an array of objects. The array is required to have an index value that will always start with zero and increase for each element in the array.

Attributes
Attribute tags are used to enhance an HTML tag. The ⟨BODY⟩ tag is considered an attribute tag because many different types of values are used to change the appearance of the Web page's body or background.

Binary code
After JavaScript code has been translated by interpretation, it becomes binary code, or machine-readable code.

Buttons
Input controls that are defined with the TYPE attribute instead of the INPUT tag.

Checkboxes
An input control that allows the user to select any or all of the listed options from a set of options.

Compiler
A highly specialized piece of software that takes a programming language that humans can understand and converts it into language computers can understand.

Components
See Controls.

Condition
Made up of two tokens and a relational operator. A conditional statement tells the browser *IF* this condition is met, perform this function; if not (*ELSE*), perform a different function.

Controls
An interactive object within a JavaScript form. Controls or components must be given a name so they can be referenced within the JavaScript code.

Cycling banner
Several graphics that are displayed one after another with a pause between images. The graphics scroll in either a fixed or random order.

Data validation
The process of checking user input data to make sure it is complete and accurate.

Decrement
To subtract one number from a value.

Event
The operating system's response to the occurrence of a specific condition.

Fonts
Also known as the style of letters, fonts determine the appearance of text in Web documents. Fonts have three attributes that can be changed—size, style, and color of text.

Function
A piece of JavaScript code that can be called upon to perform certain tasks. Functions are written by the programmer and can contain any number of JavaScript statements, including calls to other functions or methods.

.gif
An acronym for Graphics Interchange Format. Gif files are compact in size and are one of two popular graphic formats used in Web documents. The extension, .gif., helps to tell the Web browser that these files are pictures, not Web documents.

Graphics
Pictures that can be placed in Web documents.

Graphics Interchange Format
Compact graphics, often called .gif's, that are small enough in size to use in Web documents.

Hexadecimal
Hexadecimal digits operate on a base-16 number system rather than the base-10 number system most people use. Hexadecimal numbers use the letters A, B, C, D, E, and F along with the numbers 0 to 9 to create their 16 different digits.

Home page
The main Web page for a corporation, individual or organization. A home page is often the first page you see when you start your Web browser.

HTML
An acronym coming from the words Hypertext Markup Language.

HTML page
An HTML page, or HTML document, is any document created in HTML that can be displayed on the World Wide Web.

HTTP
An acronym that stands for Hypertext Transfer Protocol. On the location line in your Web browser, this is often seen in the following format: *http://www.swep.com*

Hyperlink rollover
The appearance of an image changes when the mouse pointer clicks on or moves over a hyperlink.

Hyperlinks
Allow users to click on a specific spot in a Web document and have it link to another page they've created, to another Web page on the World Wide Web, or to another spot within the current document.

Hypertext links
Used to make Web pages more interesting and easier to navigate.

Hypertext Markup Language
Tags created within a Web document that give instructions to a Web browser. These instructions determine the look and feel of a Web document on the Internet.

Hypertext Transfer Protocol
A type of digital language that Web servers use to communicate with Web browsers. A protocol is a communication system that is used to transfer data over networks.

Image
Another term used to refer to a graphic in a Web document. The letters IMG of the word are part of the HTML tag used to determine attributes of an image on the World Wide Web.

Image rollover
The appearance of an image changes when the mouse pointer moves over the image.

Increment
To add one number to a value.

Index
A variable that usually has the value of zero assigned to it. The index variable is used to access information about the array.

Instantiate
The process of creating a new object and assigning it a value.

Internet Explorer
One of two major Web browsers used to look at information on the World Wide Web. Internet Explorer was created by Microsoft Corporation and comes with every package of Windows 95, Windows 98, and Windows NT.

Interpretation
A term used by programmers to describe the line-by-line conversion process that occurs automatically at run time or when the Web browser launches the JavaScript commands that are embedded in the Web document.

Java
A programming language that creates programs called applets. Applets can be added to Web documents using tags similar to HTML tags.

JavaScript
More powerful than HTML, JavaScript allows novice Web page developers to add features to a Web document without having to know any programming language.

Joint Photographic Expert Group
Compact graphics, often called .jpeg's, that are small enough in size to use in Web documents.

.jpg or .jpeg
An acronym for Joint Photographic Expert Group. .Jpg or .jpeg files are compact in size and are one of two popular graphic formats used in Web documents. The extensions, .jpg and .jpeg, tell the Web browser that these files are pictures, not Web documents.

Keywords
A word that is recognized by the programming language as part of its language. A keyword, like IF, ELSE, or RETURN cannot be used as a variable.

Methods
Methods are specialized functions within the object, and they call upon the services of the object. A method is invoked after you type the name of the object, followed by a period.

Mosaic
The first Web browser that allowed pictures and sound to accompany text on a Web page. Mosaic was created in 1994 at the University of Illinois.

Netscape Navigator
One of two major Web browsers used on the Internet today. Navigator, created in 1995, added to the powerful features of Mosaic allowing additional features like animated graphics into a Web document.

Objects
Invisible entities that have a defined set of capabilities.

Operators
Placed between two tokens in a conditional statement.

Parameter list
A list of information that provides a programming method what it needs to perform a specific function correctly.

Programming language
A language that has to be converted from a human-readable format into machine-readable format. This process is accomplished by using a compiler to complete the operation.

Radio buttons
An input control that allows the user to select just one option from a set of options.

Real number (floating-point number)
A real number is a number that has a decimal portion.

Return value
Whenever a function is called, its name is replaced by the value it returns.

⟨SCRIPT⟩ and ⟨/SCRIPT⟩ tags
The beginning and end tags that are necessary in a Web document for a JavaScript statement to be executed. All JavaScript code must be placed within the beginning and ending tag.

Scripting language
A language that does not have to be run through a compiler for it to be understood. Web browsers will take the human-readable format and convert it into machine-readable format "on the fly."

Slide show
A collection of images that change when the user clicks on the image.

Syntax
The rules of grammar for a scripting language.

Table cell
Boxes in which you can place things to keep your Web document organized. Each table box, or cell, can have different attributes applied to text, can have a different background color, or can contain a different graphic.

Text fields
An input control that allows someone to type a string value into a specific location on a Web page.

Token
Either a variable name or a literal constant, which is followed by a relational operator. A JavaScript condition will always consist of two tokens.

Values
Value tags can be used to change the background color of a Web document. The following value tag is an example of a color value BGCOLOR=RED. Value tags are often used in conjunction with attributes. In this example, the attribute would be the ⟨BODY⟩ tag.

Variable
A name that is assigned to a literal value or to an object. Once assigned, that name can be used throughout the HTML document to refer to that particular value or object.

VRML
A language used on the World Wide Web that allows people to view and search three-dimensional landscapes and models. VRML stands for Virtual Reality Markup Language.

Web browser
Often referred to as a Web client because it allows users to interface with different operating systems and view information on the World Wide Web. It allows Web page developers to have JavaScript compiled and interpreted "on the fly."

Web page
A Web page, or Web document, is any page created in HTML that can be placed on the World Wide Web.

Web site
A Web site can include a series of Web pages that can be linked to other Web sites on the Internet. Web sites are stored on Web servers.

Webmaster
A person assigned to maintain Web pages for a Web site.

Welcome page
An introduction page when you visit a Web site on the World Wide Web. Welcome pages often include the Web page owners' e-mail address and name.

lists
    embedded and indented, 20, 22
    numbered and bulleted, 18
    ordered and unordered, 18
    parameter, 76

methods, 76
    alert ( ), 86–87
    document.write( ), 78
Mosaic, 5

Netscape Navigator, 5
numbered list, 18

objects, 76
operator, 82
ordered list, 18

pages
    home, 7
    HTML, 7, 10
    Web, 4, 7, 27
    welcome, 7
parameter list, 76
pictures, 60
programming language, 74
protocol, 38

radio buttons, 128, 129, 142
real number (floating-point
    number), 114
returns a value, 140
⟨SCRIPT⟩ and ⟨/SCRIPT⟩ tags, 75

scripting language, 74, 75
slide show, 115
spacing, 29
statement
    block, 81
    conditional, 81
status line, 90, 91
syntax, 75

table cells, 63
tables, 63
tags, 8, 30, 31, 37, 40, 66
text color, 45, 46
text fields, 128, 138
tokens, 82

unordered list, 18

values, 32, 52
variable, 102
VRML, 2

Web browser, 5, 41, 74
Web page, 4, 7, 27
    appearance, 78–79
Web site, 7
Webmaster, 5, 21
welcome page, 7
World Wide Web (WWW), 76
    communicating on, 2